DISCARDED
Goshen Public Library

GOSHEN PUBLIC LIBRARY
601 SOUTH FIFTH STREET
GOSHEN, IN 46526-3994

THE HISTORY OF CRIMINAL INVESTIGATION

IAN McKENZIE

GOSHEN PUBLIC LIBRARY
601 SOUTH FIFTH STREET
GOSHEN, IN 46526-3994

RAINTREE
STECK-VAUGHN
PUBLISHERS
The Steck-Vaughn Company

Austin, Texas

DISCARDED
Goshen Public Library

CONTENTS

4 Introduction

6 Crime and Punishment

8 Keeping the Peace

10 Identifying Criminals

12 Examining Teeth

14 Fingers and Thumbs

16 Fingerprint Records

18 Flintlocks and Early Firearms

© Copyright 1996, Steck-Vaughn Company

All rights reserved. No part of this book may be reproduced or utilized in any form or by any means, electronic or mechanical, including photocopying, recording, or by any information storage and retrieval system, without permission in writing from the Publisher. Inquiries should be addressed to: Copyright Permissions, Steck-Vaughn Company, P.O. Box 26015, Austin, TX 78755

Published by Raintree Steck-Vaughn Publishers
an imprint of Steck-Vaughn Company

Library of Congress Cataloging-in-Publication Data
McKenzie, Ian K.
    The history of criminal investigation / Ian McKenzie.
    p.   cm.—(Science discovery)
    Includes bibliographical references and index.
    Summary: Explains how various methods of identifying criminals and analyzing evidence have evolved over time.
    ISBN 0-8172-4558-8
    1. Criminal investigation—History—Juvenile literature.
    [1. Criminal investigation.]
    I. Title. II. Series.
HV8073.8.M35   1996
363.2'5—dc20   95-42014

Printed in Italy
1 2 3 4 5 6 7 8 9 0 00 99 98 97 96

Acknowledgments
AFP Photo 29, 41l; Apple Computers Ltd. 40r; Art Directors 14, 38; Forensic Science Service 24-25, 25; Ian McKenzie/Amina Memon 44; Ian McKenzie/Scotland Yard 8b; Image Select/Ann Ronan 7b, 42l; Life File 7t, 8-9, 20b, 46; Lion Laboratories plc 27; Peter Newark's Historical Pictures 6, 18t, 18b, 19l, 19r, 36; Popperfoto 12, 20t, 28, 32, 33t, 33b, 34, 37, 41r, 43; Science Photolibrary 5, 9b, 12-13, 16, 17, 21, 22, 23, 26, 26-27, 31, 39l, 39r, 40l, 42r, 45; Tony Stone 4-5, 9m, 13, 15, 35; Zefa 46-47.
Cover: Forensic scientist Francis Sheehan conducting an analysis with an electron microscope. *Courtesy of John Jay College of Criminal Justice, The City University of New York.*

20	Firearms Identification	36	Criminal Minds
22	Blood Tests	38	Genetic Fingerprints
24	Pieces of Paper	40	Databases
26	Alcohol and Other Poisons	42	Chronology of Advance
28	Examining Bones	44	Glossary
30	From Skull to Face	47	Further Reading
32	Identifying the Suspect	48	Index
34	Questioning		

INTRODUCTION

No country in the world is free of crime. There probably never has been nor ever will be such a country. But, equally, no society can exist if people can rob or steal from one another, or if people can injure, maim, or kill other people with no fear of punishment. For this reason, all nations and groups within nations have rules about what is and what is not permitted. These rules are called laws. When laws exist, a society makes arrangements to ensure that the inhabitants obey those laws. The most common method of insuring tranquility is to set up a body of people who enforce the laws and bring offenders to justice. Law enforcement officials, usually called the police, have specialist groups—detectives, or criminal investigators—that investigate crimes.

A detective, however experienced and regardless of rank, is part of a team. The team may consist of many other investigators and will involve scientists and other specialists, all of whom have one aim in mind—to collect enough evidence to justify an arrest. They must also have evidence that can be presented to a court so that a jury—or at the very least a judge—can convict a criminal based on the evidence.

The investigation team is supported by forensic scientists. Over the years, scientific discoveries have been incorporated into particular investigative techniques and procedures developed by the police. These techniques and procedures form the basis of forensic investigation.

▼ A suspect is arrested and taken to the police station for questioning.

The word *forensic* is derived from the Latin word *forensis,* meaning "giving the opportunity for debate." It has come to mean something that applies to legal debate and is usually in the form of evidence that can be presented to a court. Thus, forensic science produces scientific evidence for presentation in court. Forensic science may also be, however, the investigation and development of techniques, tests, and information-gathering strategies that will help the detectives and others involved in the prosecution. They must put together a case that will "stand up in court."

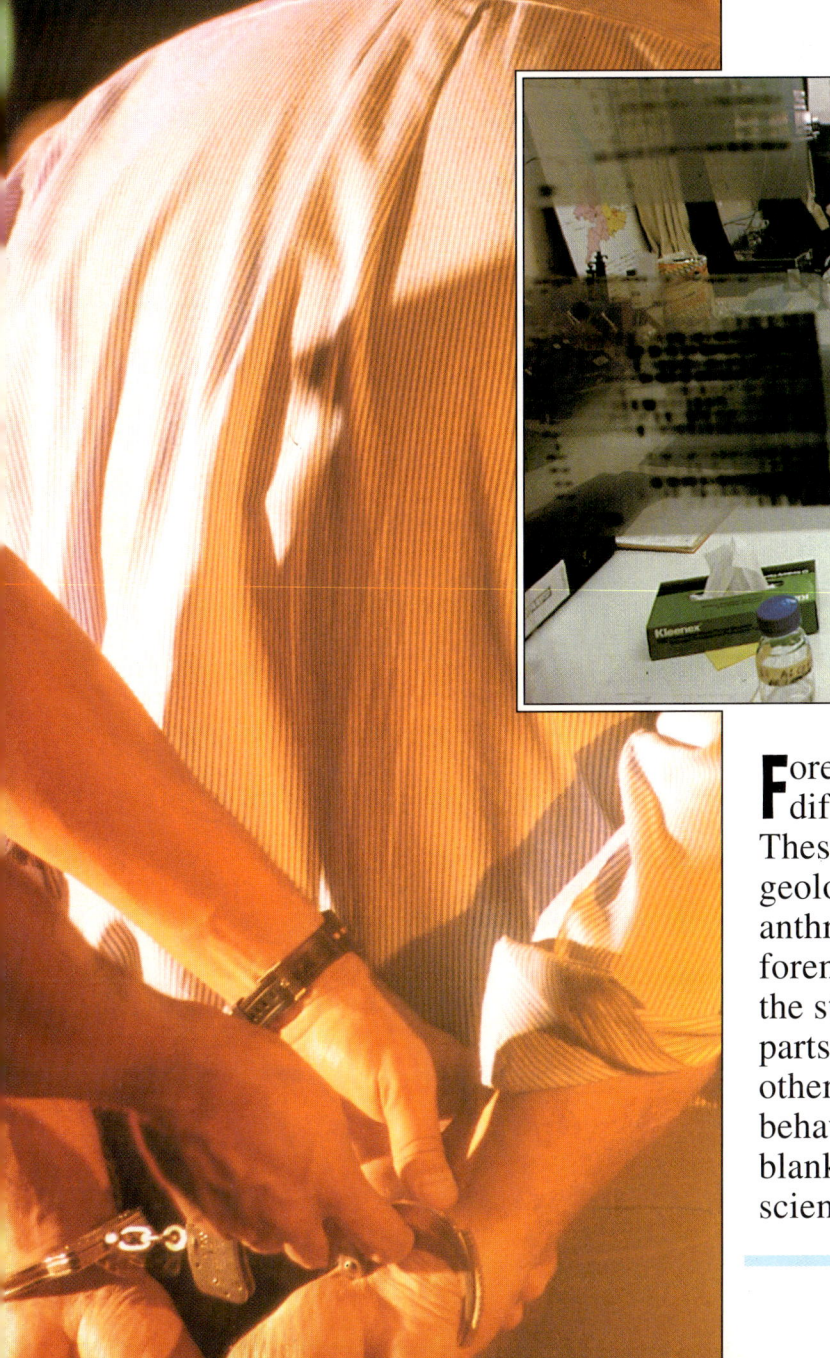

▼ **Bloodstains on clothing from a crime scene are analyzed in a forensic laboratory. One of the techniques used is genetic fingerprinting. In the picture, the dark bands on the translucent vertical screens are genetic fingerprints.**

Forensic scientists come from many different areas of scientific study. These include physics, chemistry, biology, geology, physiology, medicine, dentistry, anthropology, and psychology. In addition, forensic science includes some aspects of the study of criminology, particularly those parts that examine the causes of, or otherwise seek to explain, criminal behavior. The label *forensic science* is a blanket term covering a wide range of scientific disciplines.

CRIME AND PUNISHMENT

The Hammurabi code of Babylon (eighteenth century B.C.) was the first organized set of laws. The Ten Commandments of the Old Testament, the principles of Islam contained in the Koran, and the Mosaic law of the third century A.D. added religious principles. Roman law dates back to 753 B.C., and today in almost every industrialized society it is possible to trace the source of legal and policing systems to those of the ancient Greeks and Romans. In many countries, the legal system includes religious beliefs.

Policing in ancient times was done in some societies by soldiers, perhaps called the emperor's guard or some similar title. In others societies, the responsibility fell on the people themselves. The word *police* comes from the Latin word *polites*, meaning "citizen," conveying the idea that the police are of, or about, the people. Sometimes policing was accomplished by both soldiers and private citizens.

▶ This sixteenth-century woodcut shows a woman in a ducking stool. Women suspected of witchcraft were sometimes ducked or thrown into a deep pool of water and held under for a few minutes. If they remained conscious they were accused of being in league with the devil. Those accused of witchcraft were usually tied to a stake and burned to death.

After the withdrawal of the Romans from northern Europe about A.D. 486 and until the end of the Middle Ages around 1500, arbitrary executions were common. Many people were declared guilty of crimes following trials by ordeal. One ordeal required a person accused of theft to lift and carry for five paces a piece of metal that had been heated red-hot. If the burns healed within a given period, the accused was said to be not guilty of the crime. If the wound did not heal (there was virtually no medical knowledge at that time) or if the person refused to lift the red-hot metal, he or she was declared guilty—and was almost certainly executed. Gradually, these inhumane practices fell into disuse; but in many countries, as in ancient Rome, the idea had taken root that the people themselves were the source of law and order in their communities.

▶ Dogs can follow the trail of a person for many miles. Today, German Shepherds and Labradors are most commonly used, particularly in urban areas. However, many people still believe that the bloodhound is the best tracker. Dogs can also be trained to sniff for drugs and explosives.

▼ Louis Daguerre created the first photographs by using silver-plated sheets of copper. The sheets were made light sensitive by treating them with iodine vapor. They were put in the camera and exposed by removing the lens cap. The pictures were developed using a salt solution.

Some of the techniques now used in forensic science have been around for hundreds of years. People knew that broken pieces would fit back together. A broken tip of a knife blade might be found in a wound or lying near a dead body and then accurately matched to a broken knife. At the very least, the person in possession of the knife would have some explaining to do! Forensic scientists call this procedure mechanical fit.

Between the sixteenth century and the middle of the nineteenth century, scientists invented, designed, and developed the prototypes of many pieces of equipment essential to modern forensic science. In 1673 Antoni van Leeuwenhoek (1632–1723), a Dutchman, produced the first effective microscope. In 1728 German Johann Schultz noticed that an image of an object could be transferred to a plate coated in silver nitrate and chalk. This idea was later developed in France by Louis Daguerre (1789–1851), who created the daguerreotype, an early form of the photograph.

 # KEEPING THE PEACE

During the fifteenth and sixteenth centuries, people in Europe started to congregate in cities, and the old practice of people being solely responsible for the peacekeeping of their own locality started to disintegrate. By the start of the seventeenth century, groups of watchmen were assembled in many cities. These people, often elderly and poorly paid, would patrol the streets at night and would attempt to keep the peace.

Later, two methods of policing evolved. The first was based on military organization and practice: a body of men (there were few women in early policing systems) who were organized as though they were an army. The second was a group, sometimes called civilians in uniform, that was organized to be men of the people rather than an army of occupation. The two styles exist even today: the military style of policing (for example in France, Italy, and Pakistan), and the civilian style (for example in Great Britain and Scandinavia). In some countries the two styles exist side by side.

▲ The *caribinieri* in Chile wear military style uniforms and can easily be mistaken for army officers.

▶ This mounted policeman, on duty in Chicago, has a more relaxed appearance.

▲ Robert Peel

In 1829 Robert Peel (1788–1850), the British Home Secretary, was responsible for introducing to London what is usually considered as the first organized civilian police force—the London Metropolitan Police. Peel deliberately chose uniforms for his officers that had no resemblance to those of the army.

In some countries there are layers of law enforcement. There may be a government or federal police, a body of officers responsible for a state or province, and more local law enforcement through counties, cities, and towns. In the United States, the sheriff is a county-based law enforcement officer. The name developed from the English *shire reeve*, an official of the monarch who was responsible for the order of a county.

8

In 1910 Edmond Locard (1877–1966), a French doctor of medicine and a lawyer, was working at the University of Lyons. He proposed that, in all scientific disciplines, the idea that "every contact leaves a trace" was of particular significance. This idea had profound consequences on the development of forensic science.

At its simplest, this theory suggests that every criminal, usually unintentionally, takes something with him or her from the scene of the crime and, at the same time, leaves something at the scene. If someone is run down by an automobile, pieces of paint may be transferred from the car to the victim's clothing, and minute traces of the person's clothing, skin, or bodily fluids may be transferred to the car. This principle is known as the theory of trace evidence or sometimes as the exchange principle.

▼ **Medical evidence collected at the scene of a crime is sealed in sterile plastic bags.**

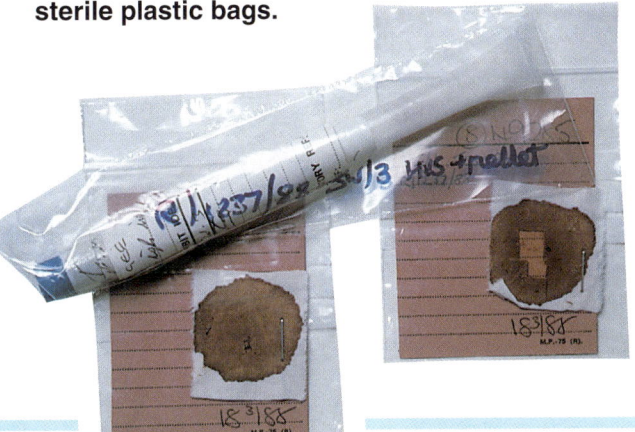

 ## CHAIN OF EVIDENCE

The exchange principle has a number of practical consequences for those collecting evidence from the scene of a crime. Not only will traces of the criminals be left at the scene, but so too will traces of the investigators—unless they are very careful.

In recent years, detectives and scientists have begun to wear overalls when investigating crime scenes. The overalls are made of a special material, often paper, that does not shed fibers and thus contaminate the scene. Investigators place everything they remove into sterile bags. Plastic bags can sweat, which could damage fingerprints, so physical evidence is usually put in paper bags. Each bag is numbered and sealed and is passed on to another person only if the person signs for it. This is because, when a trial takes place, the court must be satisfied that the item examined by the forensic scientist is the same as the one taken from the scene. These steps are called the chain of identification of evidence. The chain of evidence and the maintenance of forensic integrity are key features of modern crime-scene investigation. Only in movies do you see investigators pick up guns by sticking pencils up the barrel or wrap evidence in a handkerchief.

9

IDENTIFYING CRIMINALS

Some people commit crime after crime, undeterred by the threat of imprisonment or even of execution. Early attempts to explain this behavior included the assumption that the brains of such people were different. Perhaps their skulls were abnormal, or internal spirits drove them to commit crimes. These ideas were developed by Italian criminologist Cesare Lombroso (1836–1909) who studied more than six thousand criminals in prison. In 1876 Lombroso suggested that physical features were linked to particular types of criminal activity. For example, "…swindlers, bandits, and assassins are likely to have heads of exaggerated size," or "pickpockets have long hands, high stature, black hair, and scanty beards."

To provide data to support their arguments, Lombroso and his followers designed and built a range of measuring instruments. The craniograph was a device for accurately measuring and drawing on cardboard the shape of a person's skull. The campimeter was an instrument designed to test Lombroso's idea that some criminal types had poor eyesight. These devices provided the basis for anthropometry—the study of human body measurements, based on the idea that no two people share the same bodily statistics. But we now know that Lombroso's ideas linking physical type to crime were mistaken.

▼ **Some of Lombroso's criminal types**

"Highwaymen have thick hair and odd-shaped heads."

"Arsonists have long feet and hands, small heads, and weigh less than normal."

"Swindlers have large jaws, prominent cheekbones, pale faces, and are overweight."

"Pickpockets have long hands, high stature, black hair, and scanty beards."

Alphonse Bertillon (1853–1914) was a junior record clerk with the Sûreté, the French Criminal Investigation Bureau. To identify habitual criminals, hundreds of clerks sifted through hundreds of thousands of descriptions and drawings of people who had been arrested.

Bertillon decided to devise a system of classifying the data and images based on measurements of parts of the body. Within a year of the acceptance of his ideas by his superiors, about three hundred prisoners with previous convictions were identified as the culprits in other crimes. Bertillon became famous. Anthropometry was renamed the Bertillon system in his honor, and in 1888 he became the Director of the Judicial Identification Service of France.

▲ **Bertillon set up a system for taking measurements of criminals' bodies.**

 ## BERTILLON'S FOLLY

Bertillon was so convinced of the value of his system that he actively opposed the new science of fingerprinting (or dactylography, as it was then known). He reluctantly added fingerprinting to his measurements but he did not classify them, and saw them only at best as a supplement to his own system.

In 1911 the *Mona Lisa*, Leonardo da Vinci's famous portrait, was stolen from the Louvre Museum. Bertillon went to the gallery to supervise the investigation. Despite finding a full set of fingerprints on the picture frame, he had no way of matching them with his records.

Two years later, a man who had been arrested several times in Paris, and from whom Bertillon had taken both measurements and fingerprints, was charged with the crime. He had been arrested while smuggling the painting to Italy.

EXAMINING TEETH

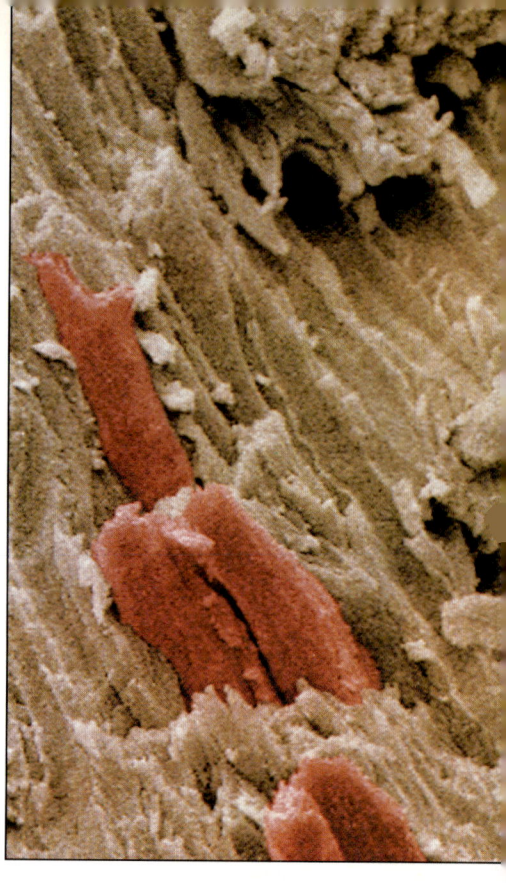

In 1447 the dead body of the French Duke of Burgundy was identified by his missing back teeth. In 1776 the body of General Joseph Warren of the U.S. Army was dug up and identified by an ivory and silver bridge that replaced a missing tooth. He had been buried by British troops after they had taken Bunker Hill on June 17, 1775 during the American Revolution (1775–1783).

Forensic dentistry is a science of comparison. If the teeth and jaw of a corpse can be matched to earlier dental records, then the corpse can be identified. Similarly, because teeth develop and wear in individual ways, a bite mark can be compared with the teeth of a suspect.

British pathologist Keith Simpson (1907–1988) developed ways of examining and comparing the teeth of a corpse or skeleton with dental records by using X rays. His work was further aided by a number of other scientific and technological advances. In 1909, American physiologist Thomas Hunt Morgan (1866–1945) established that heredity takes place through chromosomes. Chromosomes found in the nucleus of human cells are arranged in 23 pairs. The 23rd pair is different depending on whether it belongs to a man or a woman. If the pulp at the core of a tooth is exposed to ultraviolet light and the tooth is from a man, the pulp glows. If it is from a woman, it does not.

In the early 1930s two German engineers, Ernst Ruska (1906–1988) and Max Knoll, built a primitive electron microscope. The device was improved by Russian-born Vladimir Zworykin (1889-1982), working in the United States, and today the electron microscope is a critically important tool in the examination of dental and bite-mark evidence. Images and photographs can be magnified up to 150,000 times. Minute variations are clearly visible on the surface of teeth and in bite marks, allowing very fine comparisons between one surface or imprint and another.

▲ Keith Simpson arrives at a murder scene in England on December 12, 1960.

◀ **Human teeth are protected by hard, translucent enamel. Minute marks and variations in the enamel become visible under the electron microscope, allowing detailed comparison of teeth and bite marks.**

 **LEE HARVEY OSWALD**

Following the assassination of President John F. Kennedy in Dallas, Texas, in 1963, Lee Harvey Oswald, the man arrested for the shooting, was murdered. In the late 1970s rumors started to circulate that it was not Oswald who was arrested, but a Soviet spy impersonating Oswald. In 1981 Oswald's body was exhumed and a positive identification was made using Oswald's military dental records.

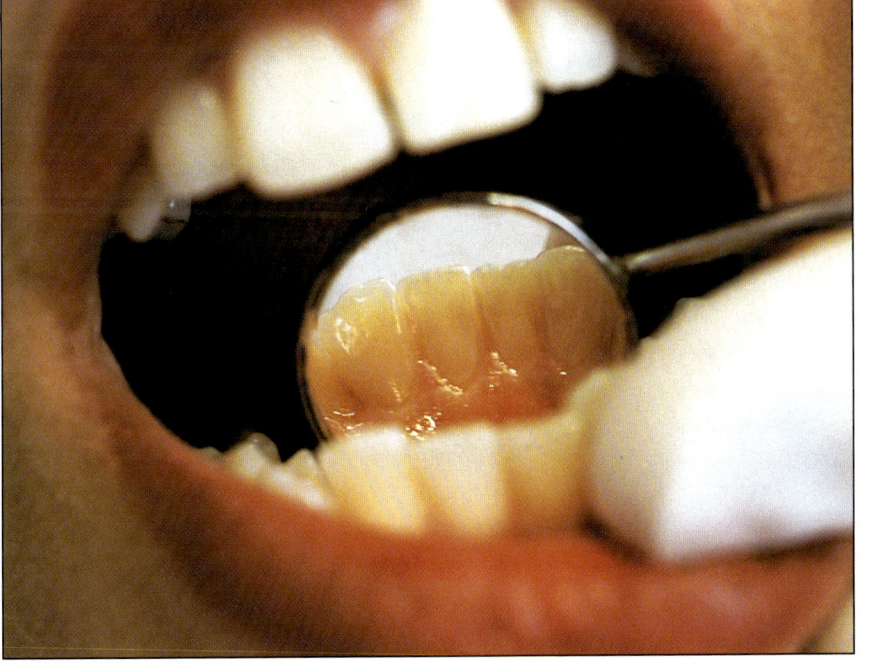

◀ **Dentists keep careful notes on their patients, regularly recording any loss or damage to their teeth and any treatment given.**

In 1906 in England, the first case went to court in which bite marks left by a suspect at the scene of a crime were used as evidence. One of two men involved in a burglary took a bite out of a piece of cheese and left the cheese at the scene of the crime! In 1948 George Gorringe was convicted of the murder of his wife, in part because of the evidence gathered by Keith Simpson, who compared a cast of the accused's teeth with a bite mark on the body. This was the first bite-mark evidence to support the conviction of a murderer in Britain. The following year Keith Simpson was asked to help the investigation of a series of murders. John George Haigh was suspected of murdering, among others, a Mrs. Durand-Deacon. Her body had disappeared, but eventually a few pieces of bone and a full set of dentures were discovered at the bottom of a vat of sulfuric acid. The dentures were identified by Mrs. Durand-Deacon's dentist. Haigh had been convinced that with no body there could be no trial. However, he was later convicted of her murder.

FINGERS AND THUMBS

Fingerprints occur because dirt, blood, and many other materials with which the fingers have come in contact are transferred to any surface touched by the fingers. Even a clean hand may be covered in salts, amino acids, and other chemical substances that are naturally produced by the skin.

Italian physiologist Marcello Malpighi (1628–1694) first described the patterns of ridges and pores on the tips of the fingers. It was part of a descriptive study of human skin, and his pioneering work was recognized by the naming of one of the nine layers of human skin as the Malpighian layer.

Although there was other work by Malpighi's contemporaries, it was not until 1823 that Jan Evangelista Purkinje (1787–1869), a Czechoslovakian physiologist, described whorls, ellipses, and triangles formed by the lines of the ridges and grooves of the surface of the skin on the fingers.

WILLIAM HERSCHEL

William Herschel (1833–1917), an English civil servant, worked in India for the British colonial government. He suspected that former soldiers, to whom he was paying pensions, were claiming more than once. They were lining up, making a mark (an *X* or some such signature), receiving the cash, and going right to the end of the line again. Herschel introduced a procedure in which the men's fingerprints were recorded on both their pay book and on the receipt form, making fraud impossible.

Herschel also showed that the grooves and ridges of the fingers do not change after the first six months following conception.

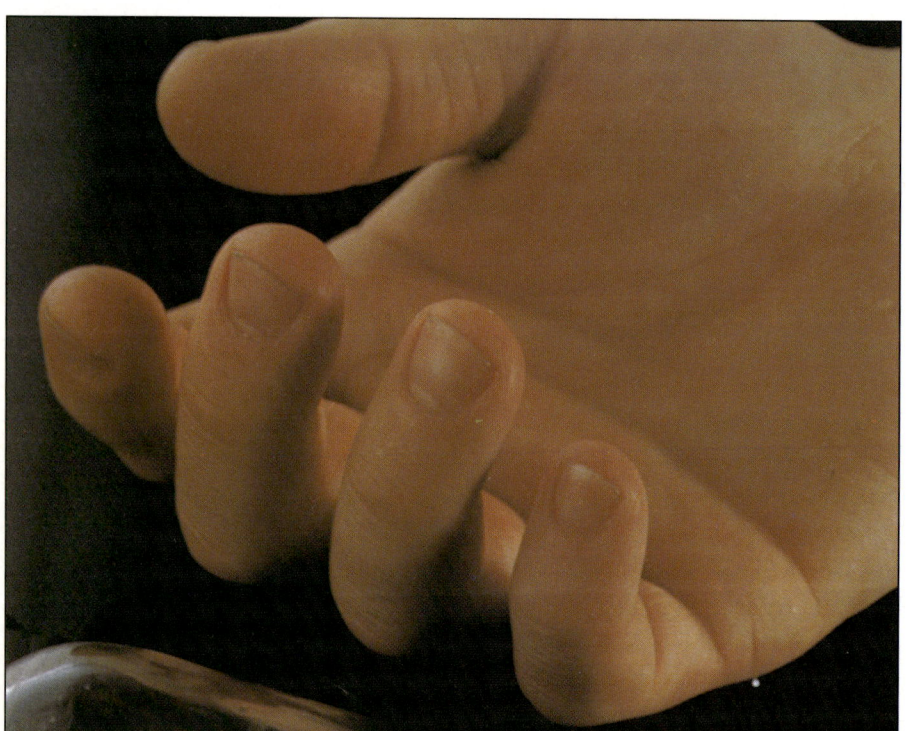

◀ The patterns of ridges on the tips of human fingers were first scientifically examined and described in the seventeenth century by Marcello Malpighi.

▲ At its simplest, a fingerprint is either an arch, a loop, or a whorl. (There is a fourth kind—a composite or compound print—which is a combination of any one with either or both of the other two.) Statisticians have estimated that 65 percent of fingerprints are loops, 5 percent are arches, and 30 percent are whorls or composites.

The first criminological use of fingerprints was made in 1880 by Henry Faulds (1843–1930), a Scottish physiologist who had been a missionary in Tokyo during the 1870s. Faulds published a paper in which he described dactylography, and discussed "…the forever unchangeable finger furrows of important criminals." Faulds's enthusiasm for dactylography was based upon success in two cases in which he had been involved in Japan. In one, following a break-in, the Tokyo police had arrested a man who fervently denied the crime. At the scene, a handprint had been found on a white wall. Faulds was able to show that this was not the same as that of the man who was in custody. Although at first the police refused to accept it, Faulds declared the man's innocence. The police changed their minds when, a few days later, another man confessed to the crime and was shown to have a palm print that matched the one on the wall.

Superficially, there seem to be millions of different patterns in the grooves, ridges, loops, whorls, and arches of the fingertips. Francis Galton (1822–1911), an English scientist, identified basic recurring shapes—the points at which the ridges run together to form a triangle, or delta. Galton published his ideas in 1892, describing four basic delta patterns: no delta, delta on the left, delta on the right, and more than one delta. He was encouraged in his efforts by an association with Alphonse Bertillon and through discussion with William Herschel about his experiences in India.

Edward Henry (1859–1931), later to become the director of the Scotland Yard fingerprint branch in Great Britain, met with Galton and added the final step to the classification process: the identification of the five patterns that are still the core of fingerprint examination to this day. These patterns are arches, tented arches, radial loops, ulna loops, and whorls. The Galton-Henry system went into operation at Scotland Yard in June 1900.

FINGERPRINT RECORDS

One of the first things that Edward Henry did on his appointment to Scotland Yard in 1901 was to set up fingerprint records for all criminals sentenced to more than one month's imprisonment. In 1902 Harry Jackson became the first person to be convicted in Great Britain because of fingerprint evidence. Jackson, a burglar, left a fingerprint in wet paint at the scene of his crime.

In 1911, in the United States, Thomas Jennings appealed his conviction on charges of murder. Jennings had been involved in a bungled burglary and had left a perfect impression of four fingers of his left hand at the crime scene. The impression perfectly matched Jennings's fingerprints already in police records. The Illinois Supreme Court ruled that there was a sound scientific basis for allowing the use of fingerprints as evidence, and that Jennings's death sentence should stand.

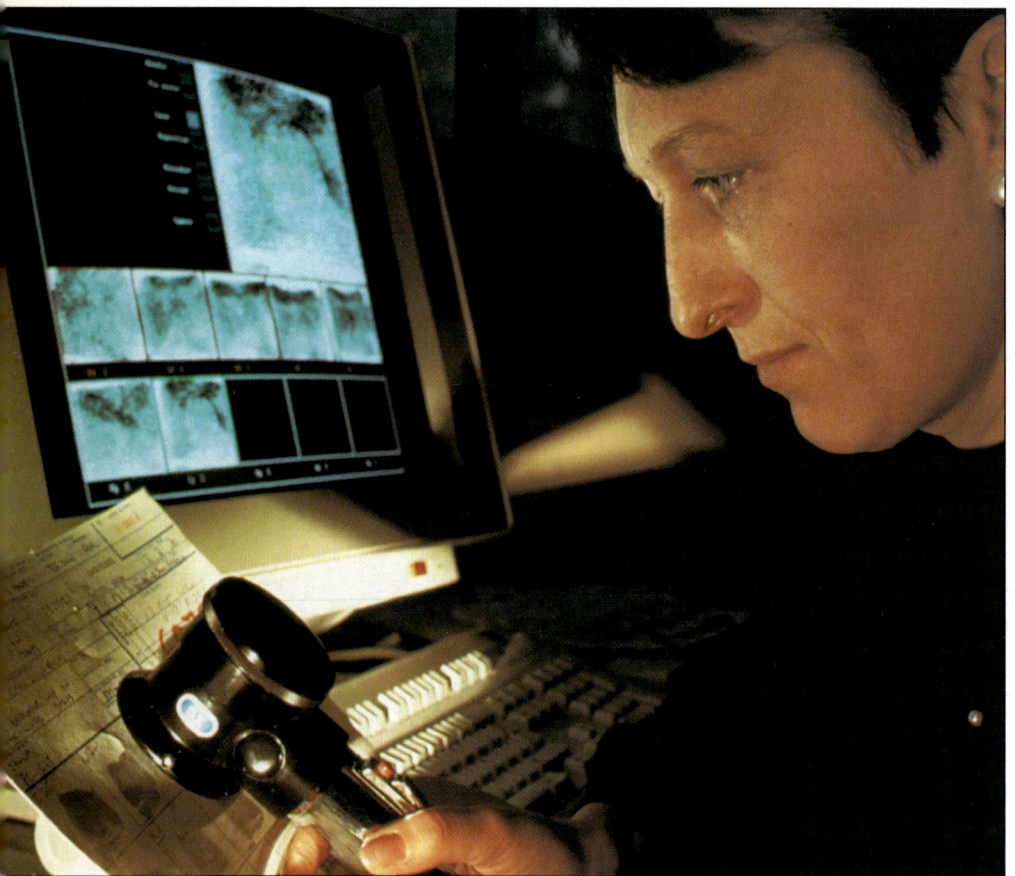

▶ Computer matching of fingerprints digitally compares prints obtained from a crime scene with prints held in police records. A split screen shows the prints side by side, and a comparison program checks both prints. In this case the prints are identical.

◀ Old paper copies of criminals' fingerprints are transferred to a computer system using a handheld scanner.

Fingerprints at the scene of a crime are exposed in a number of ways, some of which have remained unchanged since they were introduced by Edward Henry in the early part of the twentieth century. The most common are dusting smooth, firm, and light-colored surfaces with fine carbon powder (vegetable black) and dark surfaces with aluminum or lanconide (white) powder. The powders stick to the surface of the marks, making them visible. Iodine and other chemicals might be used to reveal marks on rough or problem surfaces.

In 1960 Theodore Maiman (1927–) of the Hughes Research Laboratory in Miami produced the first laser. Laser light can be used by forensic scientists to flood a room, causing chemicals in any fingerprints to fluoresce. During the 1980s, investigators discovered by accident that the vapor from superglue reacts with chemicals in human sweat and produces a white image of fingerprints.

X-RAY FINGERPRINTS

X rays were first discovered in 1895 by German physicist Wilhelm Conrad Röntgen (1845–1923). X rays are a form of radiation that will pass through soft human tissue but not through other substances, such as lead. A British father and son team, William Henry Bragg (1862–1942) and William Lawrence Bragg (1890–1971), shared a Nobel prize in physics in 1915 for discovering that X rays fired at crystals are scattered in specific patterns that can be captured on photographic plates. In the 1960s Daniel Graham and Hugh Gray, radiographers at the Glasgow Victoria Infirmary in Scotland, devised a system in which a beam of X rays is aimed at human skin that has been dusted with lead powder. The electrons released from the lead produce an image on X-ray film. Dusting and X-raying fingers provided a more accurate means of recording fingerprints.

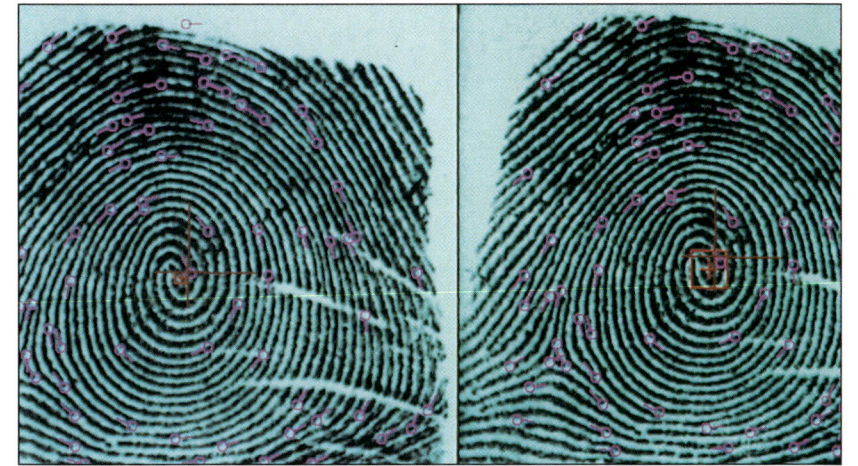

Fingerprint experts try to assess how closely fingerprint samples match fingerprints on record. These similarities are called the points of reference. Experts in different countries differ over the number of points of reference required to prove beyond any doubt that a fingerprint left at the scene of a crime matches that of a suspect. In France 17 are required; in Great Britain 16; Greece, Switzerland, and Spain 12; and India 8 to 12, depending on the area. In the United States, following a report by an eminent committee in 1973, a formal minimum standard was abandoned. Prosecutors are now required to convince the jury of the importance of fingerprints found.

 # FLINTLOCKS AND EARLY FIREARMS

The inventor of gunpowder and the designer of the first gun probably lived in China in the third century A.D. Almost all modern firearms are basically similar in design to early weapons. Each has a tube, a projectile, and an explosive charge. At first, firearms were loaded by ramming gunpowder down the barrel from the front. A wad of paper or cotton was inserted, followed by a pellet and another wad of paper. To fire the weapon a fuse was lit. Later, flintlocks were fired by striking a flint with metal to make a spark.

 **TELLING TALES**

In 1794 a British doctor dressing the bullet wound of a Lancashire man found a wad of paper in the wound. The paper had been torn from a ballad sheet and had been used when the gunpowder was loaded down the muzzle of the gun. The remainder of the torn paper was found in the pocket of the main suspect.

In two similar instances, wads of paper were key features in solving murders. The first, in Great Britain in 1854, involved a piece of the London *Times* newspaper; and the second, in France in 1891, part of the French journal *Lorraine Almanche*.

▲ A flintlock pistol made in London by James Barbar in 1715

▶ A soldier using an early firearm from Jacques de Gheyn's *Manual of Arms*, 1607

Early firearms were inaccurate because their barrels were smooth inside. Rifling was first used in the sixteenth century. A number of parallel spiral grooves were made along the inside of the gun barrel. The weapon was loaded from the back with a bullet made of malleable material slightly larger in diameter than the barrel. As the bullet traveled down the barrel, the rifling cut into the soft material and made the bullet spin. The spin of the bullet made the aim of the gun more accurate.

18

American inventor Samuel Colt (1814–1862) took out his first patent on a revolver in 1836. He developed the six-shooter and metal cartridges. Cartridges today are usually made of brass and hold a charge of gunpowder and a bullet. When the trigger is pulled, a pin strikes the bottom of the cartridge, the gunpowder explodes, and the bullet is shot down the gun barrel. The first smokeless gunpowder was developed by Alfred Nobel (1833–1896), Swedish inventor and founder of the Nobel prizes, in 1887. This reduced the smoke cloud produced when a gun was fired.

▲ Samuel Colt was born in Hartford, Connecticut, and ran away to sail the seas in 1827. He later returned to Connecticut to open a gun factory.

▲ The Colt New Model Army Revolver of 1860 was the principal handgun used during the Civil War (1861–1865).

As a bullet travels down a barrel, tiny imperfections in the rifling become etched into the bullet. These imperfections are unique to the gun, which means that the rifling marks on a spent cartridge produce a kind of fingerprint linking the cartridge to the gun. During a murder investigation in France in 1889, Alexandre Lacassagne (1844–1921) used this special application of Locard's exchange principle to match a bullet from the murder scene with a gun belonging to the main suspect. Small deformations of the firing pin also become etched into the bottom of the cartridge case. Some modern weapons have a device, called an extractor claw, that removes a spent cartridge case from the weapon and casts it to one side before another cartridge, complete with bullet and primer, is automatically inserted into the breech. The action of the claw also leaves identifiable marks on the bullet casing.

FIREARMS IDENTIFICATION

Throughout the nineteenth and twentieth centuries, most of the development of firearms and ammunition occurred in the United States. In 1923 Charles Waite and Philip Gravelle set up the Bureau of Forensic Ballistics (BFB). Later they were joined by Colonel Calvin Goddard, a former doctor, whom many people regard as the world's first true ballistics expert. Gravelle and Goddard developed their own specialized equipment, most importantly the comparison microscope around 1921. This was basically two separate microscopes joined by an optical bridge, allowing two objects to be compared. Modern comparison microscopes allow the two objects to be rotated, moved independently, and viewed together on a computer screen.

Also in the early 1920s, another American, John Fischer, invented the helixometer. This device, a hollow probe fitted with a light and magnifying lenses, was used to examine the inside of gun barrels. Today, probes with fiber-optic filaments give high-quality images on computer screens.

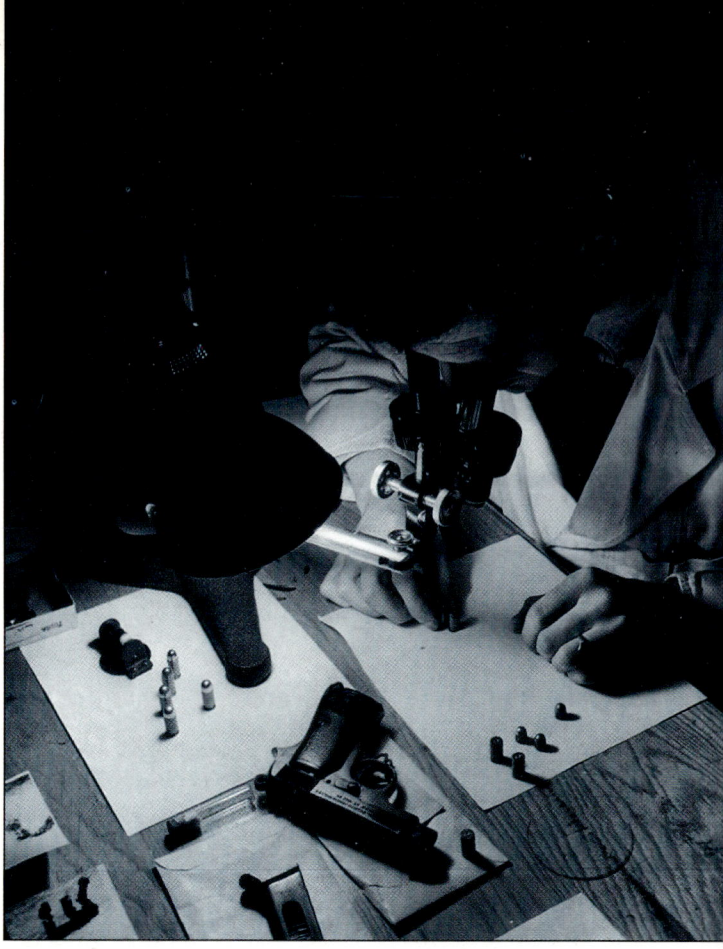

▲ A forensic scientist examines bullets under a comparison microscope to discover whether they were fired from the same weapon.

▼ Weapons are tested in specially constructed firing ranges. The spent bullets are collected and examined in a forensic laboratory.

In the early 1930s Gerald Burrard, an English ballistics expert, devised a way to obtain test bullets by firing weapons into a water tank. Bullets only travel a few inches in water, regardless of their previous speed, and can easily be recovered from the bottom of the tank. Water tanks are particularly useful today for obtaining test firings from weapons, such as machine guns and machine pistols, capable of discharging dozens of rounds with one brief squeeze of the trigger.

Ballistics is the study of the flight paths of bullets. The flight of a bullet is known as the trajectory. Trajectories can be calculated in a number of ways. In a relatively enclosed space, provided the position and alignment of the gun is known, a straight line can be drawn along the bullet's projected flight path to the place where the bullet might be found. At simple crime scenes, detectives usually mark supposed and actual trajectories with lengths of string. A small handheld laser may also be used. However, once a bullet enters a human body, it can behave in very strange ways, making trajectory predictions difficult.

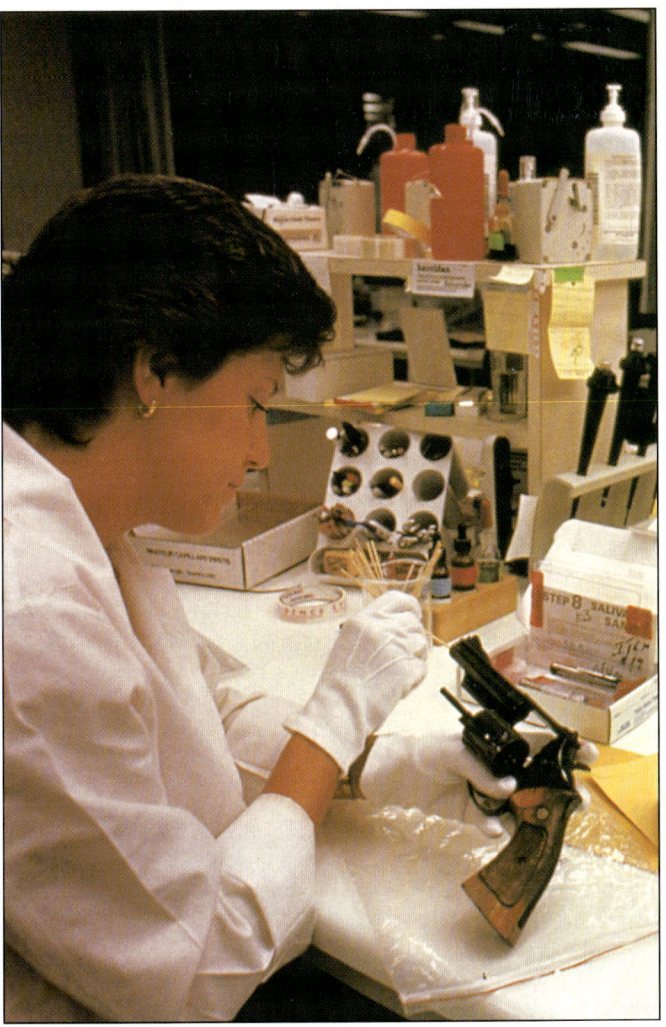

 ## THE MAGIC BULLET

After President John F. Kennedy was assassinated in Dallas on November 22, 1963, there was much discussion about what has come to be known as the magic bullet. The rifle fire that hit Kennedy in the neck apparently passed into the shoulder and out the elbow of Texas Governor John Connally, who was seated in front of him. Some people have claimed that this trajectory was not possible with the type of rifle and ammunition used. Because of this, it has been suggested that there were two different shots from two different gunmen. After more than 30 years of debate, the magic bullet still has not been explained to everyone's satisfaction.

◀ **A forensic scientist examines a handgun for traces of blood at the Federal Bureau of Investigation (FBI) laboratory in Washington, D.C.**

21

BLOOD TESTS

Ancient Greek physicians believed that human blood was a source of emotion, and we still speak of people being hot-blooded, meaning that they are impetuous and emotional. It was not until 1628 that William Harvey (1578–1657), an English physician, showed that the blood circulates through the body.

At the start of the twentieth century, scientists still did not know why the blood from one person often became lumpy when mixed with the blood from another. In 1901 Austrian biologist Karl Landsteiner (1868–1943) was able to show that the presence or absence of two factors which he called A and B, and the presence or absence of two types of coagulating agents, which he also called A and B, controlled whether or not blood from two different people would mix.

By 1910 the four main blood types had been identified: A, B, AB, and O. In 1927 Landsteiner and his colleagues defined further secondary types, and later experiments isolated the rhesus factor, subdividing the main types into rhesus positive and rhesus negative. Scientists now had a reliable way of classifying human blood.

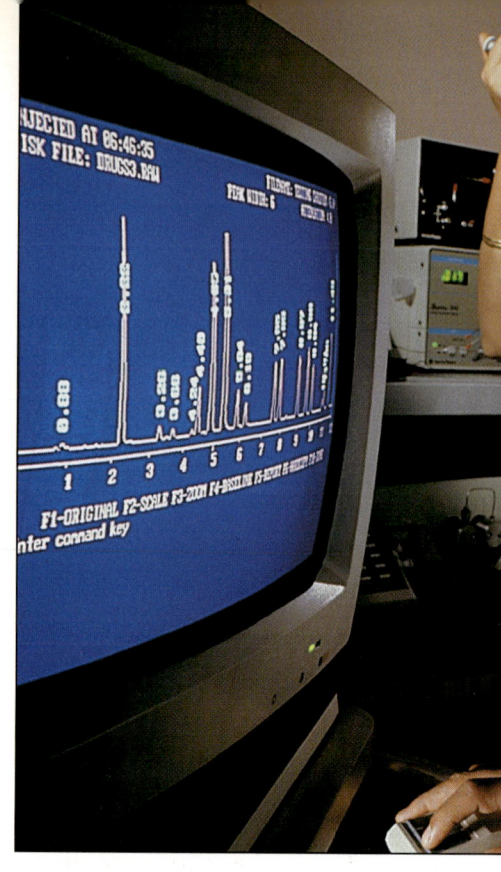

▲ High performance liquid chromatography (HPLC) is used to check substances in blood samples. These appear as peaks on the computer screen.

▶ A minute amount of a liquid sample is sucked into a syringe and injected into the top of the chromatography column. As the liquid passes down the column, it separates into its different components. These can be measured.

Blood Type	Red Cell Antigen A	Red Cell Antigen B	Plasma Antibody A	Plasma Antibody B
A	✔	✘	✘	✔
B	✘	✔	✔	✘
AB	✔	✔	✘	✘
O	✘	✘	✔	✔

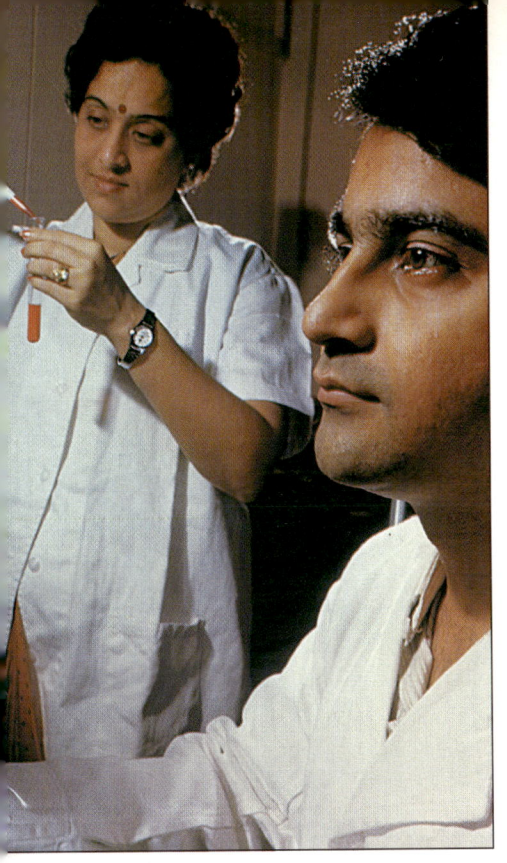

About 1880 Alexandre Lacassagne suggested that examination of the smearing and staining of blood at a crime scene could provide important trace evidence. About 1925 John Glaister (1892–1971), a Scottish pathologist, identified five patterns of bloodstains: drops, splashes, spurts, smears, and trails. In an echo of Locard's exchange principle, he proposed that such patterns could be used to re-create what happened at the scene of a crime. Clearly, it is important to link blood traces to the person they came from.

The development of spectroscopy greatly helped in analyzing minute traces of blood and other materials. In 1666 British scientist Isaac Newton (1642–1727) discovered that white light splits into a spectrum of colors when it passes through a prism. In 1859 Gustav Kirchhoff (1824–1887), a German physicist, and Robert Bunsen (1811–1899), a German chemist, began work on the idea that when heated substances give off a spectrum of light that is typical of the elements contained in the sample. Spectroscopy developed rapidly. Forensic scientists today can rely on fast, accurate analyses using emission spectroscopy and another technique, called chromatography, in which the components of substances are identified.

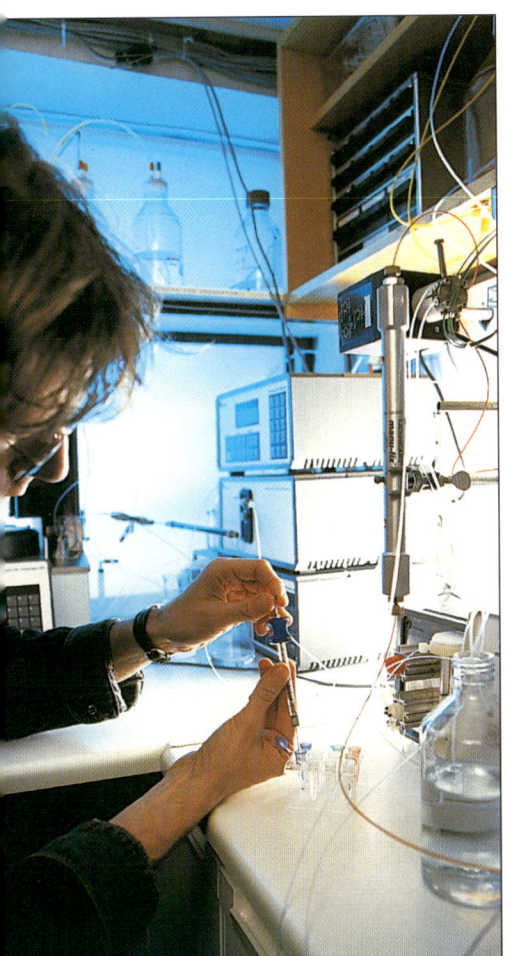

 ## HOW BLOOD TYPES MIX

Today we know that blood consists of red blood cells, white blood cells, platelets, and plasma. The plasma is a watery fluid in which the cells and platelets float. The surface of red blood cells can contain proteins, called antigens. The red cells in blood type A have the antigen A.

White blood cells produce antibodies to fight infections, and they work by homing in on the antigens on the surface of an invading infection. In fact, they home in on any antigens that invade the blood. People with blood type A don't make antibodies against A antigens. But if antigens from another type are introduced, the white cells will immediately make antibodies to destroy those antigens.

Blood type O has no antigens, so in theory anyone can safely be given type O blood, though in practice other factors have to match. People with blood type AB have both A and B antigens. Scientific studies have suggested that about 42 percent of people have type A, 9 percent have type B, 46 percent have type O, and only 3 percent have type AB.

23

PIECES OF PAPER

Edmond Locard was one of the first forensic scientists to develop expertise in both handwriting analysis and chemical methods of ink analysis. When handwriting is disputed or needs to be identified, experts compare it with a number of "control" samples. Although forgers may copy the general shape of letters, the incidentals such as slant, the way in which words or sentences start, and how the letters are connected to one another are much more difficult to copy. A comparison is made using a piece of equipment called a comparison projector. In a sense this is much like the comparison microscope, described on page 20. In this case, however, the images are projected so that they can be superimposed, one on the other, and the slant, shape, connectors, and other incidentals can be directly compared.

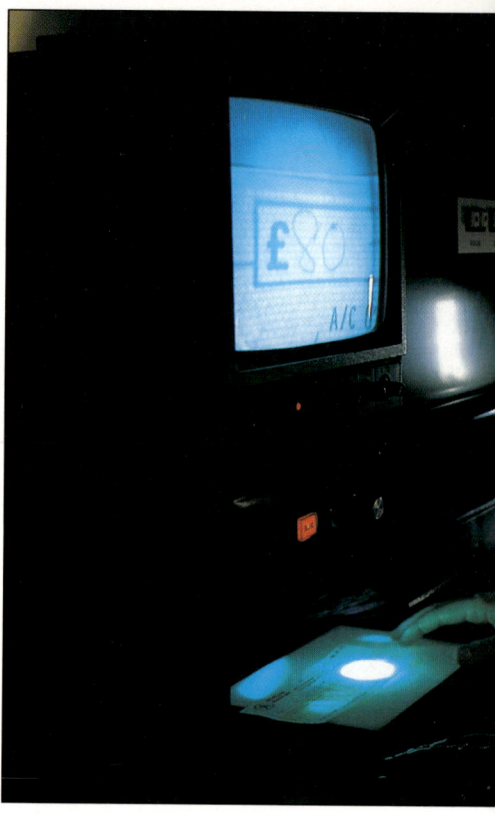

▲ The writing on a check can be verified by using ultraviolet light to expose any alterations.

Invisible radiation is another useful tool for forensic scientists examining documents. In the 1670s Christiaan Huygens (1629–1695), a Dutch physicist, suggested that light travels in waves. In 1804 German physicist Johann Ritter (1776–1810) discovered ultraviolet (UV) light. This is radiation similar to light but with a wavelength below the range of human vision. UV light allows chemical reactions that otherwise would not occur to take place and can show up things that are invisible to the naked eye. Modern handwriting experts use UV light to expose erasures and blemishes in disputed documents.

X rays have an even shorter wavelength than ultraviolet light. Using the technique for producing X-ray images of fingerprints (see page 17), Daniel Graham and Hugh Gray developed a procedure called electron-autography, which produces X-ray images of fingerprints and writing impressed under stamps and inside envelopes.

If there is a piece of paper underneath one that is being written on, impressions of the handwriting are left on the lower piece of paper. Indented impressions can be very useful in an investigation when pages have been torn from account books or personal diaries. The simplest method of showing the impressed writing is to shine a light across the surface of the paper and to photograph the result.

In the late 1970s scientists realized that impressions left on a piece of paper alter the electrical qualities of the surface of the paper. Using this information, Bob Freeman (1946–) and Doug Foster (1946–), working at the London School of Printing in 1978, developed the Electro-Static Detection Apparatus (ESDA). A piece of paper that has been electrostatically charged is sprinkled with a mixture of photocopy toner (carbon) and fine glass beads. Any impressed writing on the paper stands out because the carbon sticks to it. Legibility depends on the depth of the impression. Even where there is no visible impression, handwriting has been exposed using this method.

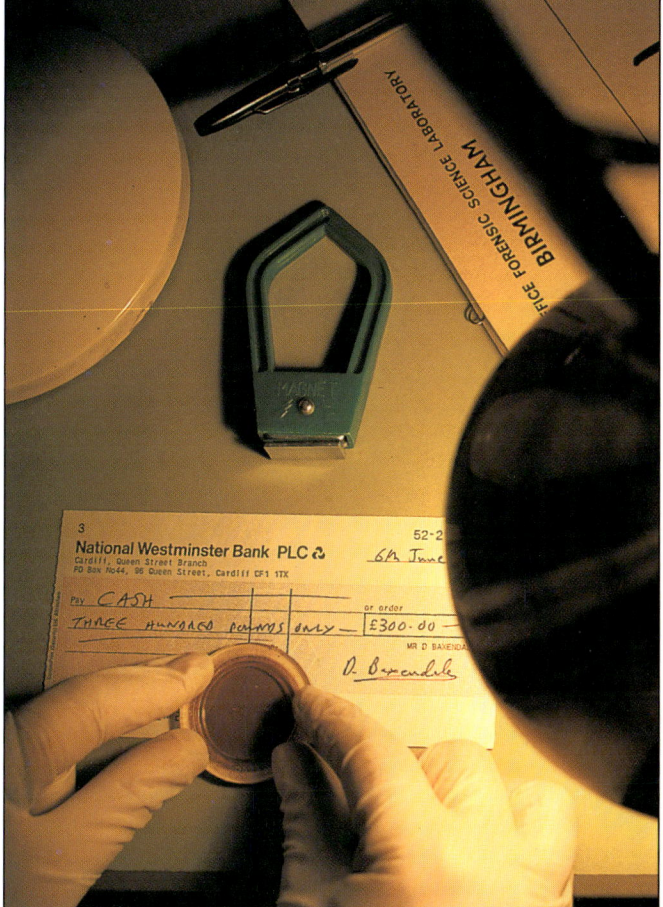

◀ A forensic scientist examines the account number on a bank check to make sure it is genuine.

 REVEALING BLANK PAGES

William Podmore was found guilty of the murder of a man named Vivian Messiter in Great Britain in 1930. The conviction was based in part on photographic evidence that showed an impression of Podmore's handwriting on the blank page of a receipt book from which the nine previous pages had been torn. Podmore, an employee of Messiter's, had been preparing false receipts for items not sold and claiming the commission. When Messiter discovered the fraud, Podmore killed him.

ALCOHOL AND OTHER POISONS

People have murdered with poisons for thousands of years. When poison may have been used, the forensic scientist analyzes the blood, body fluids, and tissue of the victim to find the exact cause of death. As long ago as 1814, in his work *Traité de Poisons*, Matthieu Orfila (1787–1853), a Spanish chemist, published a system for classifying poisons. Later, in 1836, Alfred Taylor expanded this classification and developed techniques of drug and poison identification. In the same year James Marsh developed a test for identifying the poison arsenic in human tissue.

Dozens of tests and procedures now exist to identify particular drugs and toxins. Some procedures, such as mass spectrometry, are incredibly sensitive. The first mass spectrometer was built by British scientist Francis Aston (1877–1945), who used it to research the isotopic structure of elements and for which he was awarded a Nobel prize in chemistry in 1922. The machine analyzes components by their mass and was soon adapted to analyze minute samples of drugs and blood. In nearly all countries in the world, it is a crime to sell or manufacture certain kinds of drugs and other dangerous substances without a license. In many places unlawful possession of drugs is severely punished—sometimes by execution. Sensitive, reliable tests are of vital importance.

▲ Attempts have been made, with some success, to analyze the blood of mummies that have been entombed for thousands of years.

▶ A scientist injecting a sample into a mass spectrometer. The components in the sample appear as peaks on the computer screen.

26

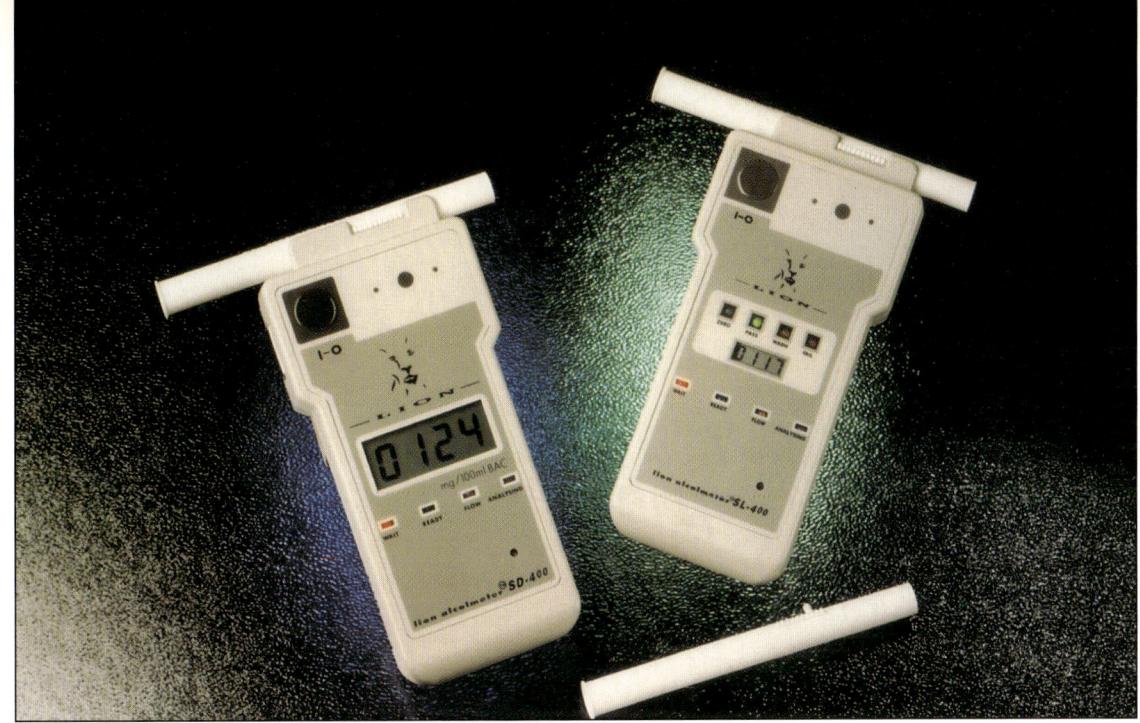

▲ The Lion Alcometer 400 series, produced by Lion Laboratories in Wales, is one of the latest sophisticated breath-alcohol measuring devices.

Alcohol is another dangerous substance. Consumed in large quantities, it is poisonous and can cause death; but even very small amounts impair the senses and affect behavior. In many countries, driving a vehicle after drinking alcohol is a crime. In the United States 80 milligrams or more of alcohol in 100 milliliters of blood is considered evidence of intoxication and will result in arrest. In some places, such as the Scandinavian countries and Japan, any alcohol at all found in the bloodstream while driving a motor vehicle will result in a conviction.

Blood samples are analyzed for alcohol content using mass spectrometry, but alcohol level is usually measured in the breath. In the past, suspected drunk drivers were asked to blow into a Breathalyzer—a glass tube containing a crystalline chemical that turned from yellow to green when there was alcohol in the breath. If the green tinge passed beyond a critical mark on the tube, the person would be arrested. Today the police are more likely to use an instrument such as the Lion Alcometer. This contains a fuel cell that converts chemical energy into an electrical charge. Alcohol in the breath is the energy source, and the electrical current activates either a pass or a fail light.

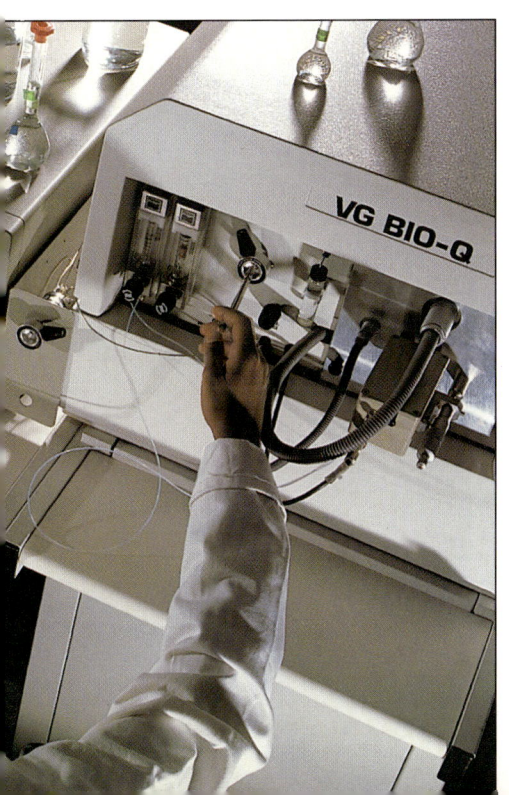

The Intoximeter, first patented in the United States in the 1980s, is a much larger and more sophisticated machine. It produces a very precise analysis of the alcohol content of the breath.

EXAMINING BONES

Records show that physicians in Alexandria, Egypt, in the third century B.C. dissected corpses in an effort to understand disease. In A.D. 1284 a book called the *Hsi Yuan Lu* was published in China. It included, among other information, descriptions of people who had died from drowning and strangulation. The book also contained details of the injuries, including bone injuries, likely to be caused by particular types of weapons.

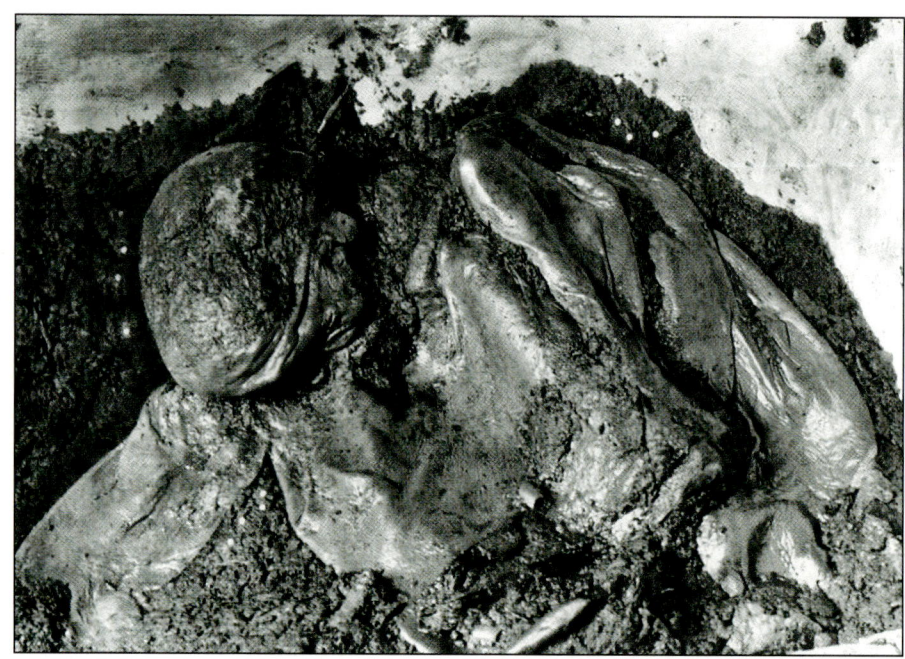

▶ In August 1984 a man's body was found in a peat bog in Cheshire, England. Scientists were able to show that the man died about 2,500 years ago of strangulation by a horsehair cord, the remnants of which were still around his neck.

In 1957 two American pathologists, Thomas McKern and Thomas Stewart, identified the stages through which the skeleton passes as a human male ages. This knowledge is the basis for identification of corpses and skeletal remains. In the 1970s the American Board of Forensic Anthropology proposed a series of procedures that aims to answer a list of questions. First, are the bones human or animal? If they are human, when did the person die? Was the person male or female, and how old was he or she at the time of death? Finally, what was the height and build of the person and his or her ethnic origin? Forensic anthropologists might look for the existence of illnesses and disorders, such as cancer or an unbalanced diet, that might have affected the structure of the bones. They will also look for wounds, fractures, and evidence of operations.

The age of a person at death can never be more than a guess if only the bones are left, but some accuracy is possible. The teeth of a person under 25 years old can be a positive guide. Changes in bone structure, particularly bone diseases and disorders such as arthritis, may also be a guide to age. The skull can be a good guide because the plates of bone that make up the cranium move together at a known, if slightly variable, rate. An examination of the main arteries, if they still exist, will give clues about age, because these degenerate.

Establishing the gender of the person is not as difficult. Not only are the bones of the pelvis slightly different in males and females, but also there are slight differences in the shape of the skull. In males, for example, the bony ridge above the eyes (the supraorbital ridge) tends to be more prominent than in females. Similarly, there are differences in the back of the skull (the nuchal crest).

▶ On September 9, 1991, a German couple, hiking in Austria, found a human body poking out of the ice of a glacier. The body had been preserved in the ice for more than five thousand years.

▼ Scientists were able to show that the body was a man between 25 and 30 years old, about five feet two inches tall, and weighing about 110 pounds. They were able to reconstruct the way the Iceman may have looked.

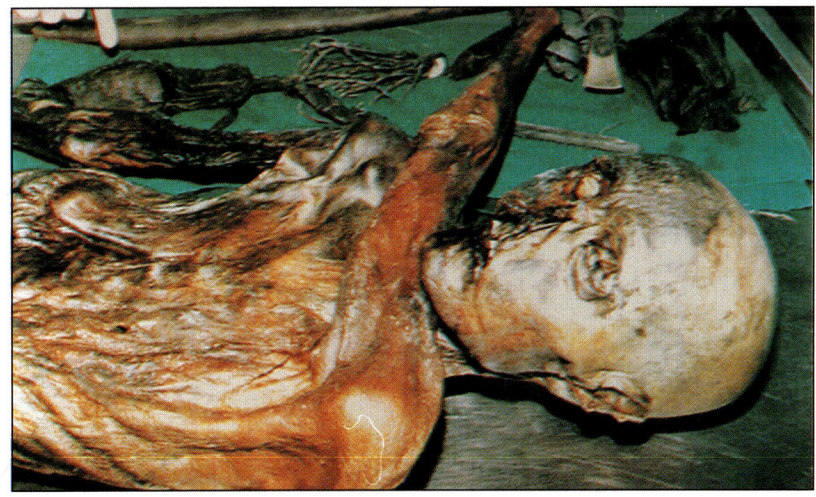

The height of the person can be estimated to within plus or minus one inch by reference to known information about the relationship of physical height to the length of the long leg bones—the femur and the tibia. These data can also provide some information about the gender of the corpse.

Anthropometric measurements can be used to distinguish one ethnic group from another, as can the shape of the skull, the layout of the teeth, and the shape of the face.

FROM SKULL TO FACE

During the 1920s Mikhail Gerasimov, a Russian paleontologist, found a way to assess the thickness of the muscle, flesh, and skin to be expected at any point over the whole of the skull. Using data gathered from the study of the heads of corpses made available to the Third Medical University College in Moscow, Gerasimov studied the relationship between the skull and the muscles, fibers, and tendons that connect to one another and to the skin covering the head and face. Between 1927 and 1930, Gerasimov used his procedure to reconstruct the facial appearance of the fossilized remains of early humans.

Gerasimov's system was refined in Great Britain in the 1980s by Richard Neave in the Department of Anatomy at Manchester University Medical School. In 1990, after the discovery of an unidentified female body, a skull cast was sent to him for reconstruction. The remains arrived in Manchester as "Little Miss Nobody." After Neave had worked on her skull cast, she was identified as Karen Price, and two men were later convicted of her murder.

▼ The stages used to reconstruct the face of the Iceman, whose body was found in an Austrian glacier in 1991.

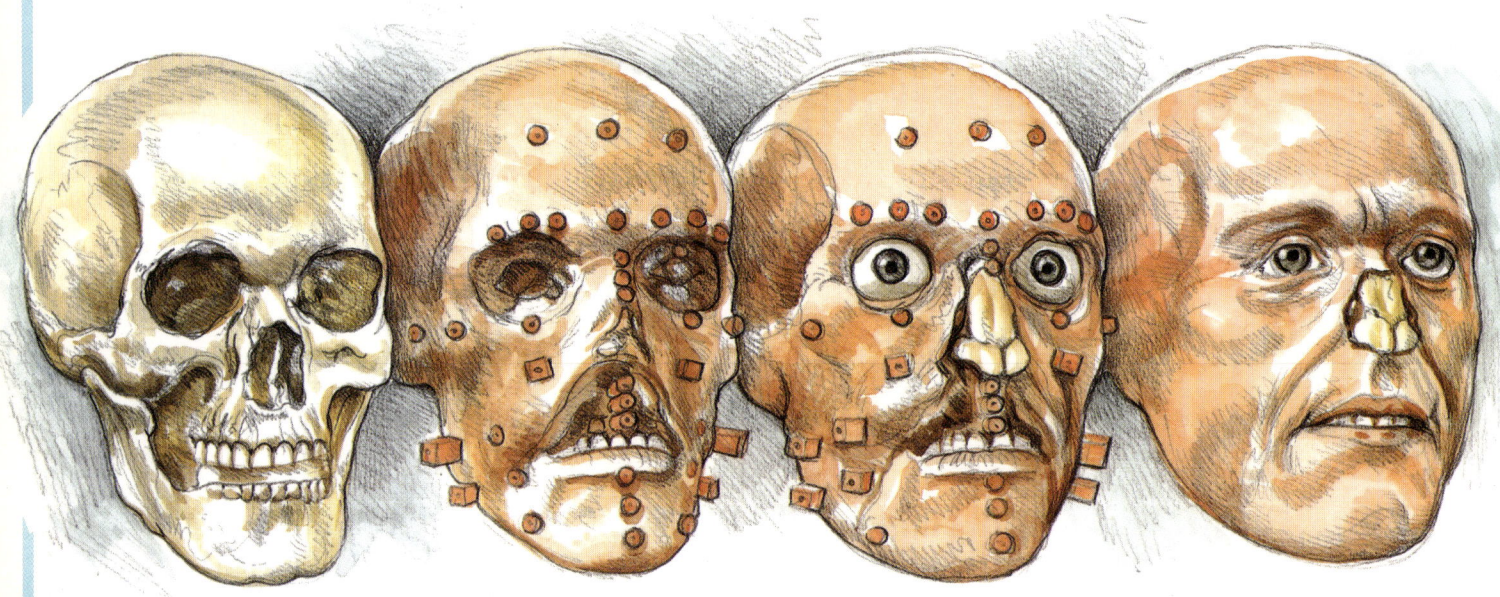

GERASIMOV'S METHOD

Gerasimov's system is deceptively simple. First a cast of the skull is made and the eye sockets are filled with false eyeballs. Then a series of very small holes are drilled at precise positions at various points on the skull cast. Small pieces of wood are inserted into the holes, the tops of the sticks matching precisely the expected depth of body tissue at that point.

Layers of modeling clay are placed over the skull cast to the exact height of the sticks. Modeling begins with the jaw and the neck and is followed by the cheeks, the temples, the mouth, and the eyes. The shape of a person's nose is determined by cartilage, which decomposes rapidly, so there is some guesswork over its reconstruction. On the other hand, much depends upon the expertise of the specialist, who uses both the skills of an artist and those of an anthropologist.

As layer after layer of material is built into the model and skin is added in the form of thin strips, the image of a person, perhaps of someone long dead, appears. Some additional guesswork may be necessary with things like the ears and the hair. But in the end there is a face that shows how the dead person might have looked. Many identifications have been made on the basis of such reconstructions.

▲ **A sculptor works on the finer details of a model head of an unidentified corpse.**

In 1991 a team of anthropologists and physicians working at the Medical Physics Department of University College Hospital in London announced a new technique: laser facial reconstruction. The procedure, developed by Robin Richards and his colleagues, was based on equipment used to predict the outcome of facial surgery. In its forensic science application, a skull (or skull cast) is put on a rotating plinth. A low-power laser beam is reflected off the skull and onto a video camera linked to a computer. The computer contains information about skull and tissue shapes, and it creates a mathematical model of the facial appearance of the unidentified person. On the output side of the computer, a machine cuts a three-dimensional model of the face and head in Styrofoam. Final touches—including perhaps the nose, ears, and hair—are added by a sculptor.

IDENTIFYING THE SUSPECT

In the 1940s Hugh McDonald was the head of the civilian division of the Los Angeles Police Department. He was dispatched to Europe to track down a number of criminals, and because he found that the descriptions given by people were both vague and incomplete, he started making rough sketches of the suspects. To save time he drew some of the facial features, such as eyes, noses, and face shapes, on transparent sheets and invited people to select those that most accurately matched the person they were seeking to describe.

Later, after considerable consultation, McDonald developed the first Identikit field pack. This consisted of coded and numbered drawings of single facial features reproduced on transparent sheets. The drawings included eyes, noses, lips, chins, mustaches, and beards, but did not include ears, because McDonald believed "…victims of crime, especially crimes of violence…never see…ears properly."

One of the advantages of McDonald's system was that the various features were identified by codes that could be telephoned to an office thousands of miles away. Using the codes and the Identikit the picture could be re-created easily. Today, however, a drawing or photograph can be sent by fax machine or by computer.

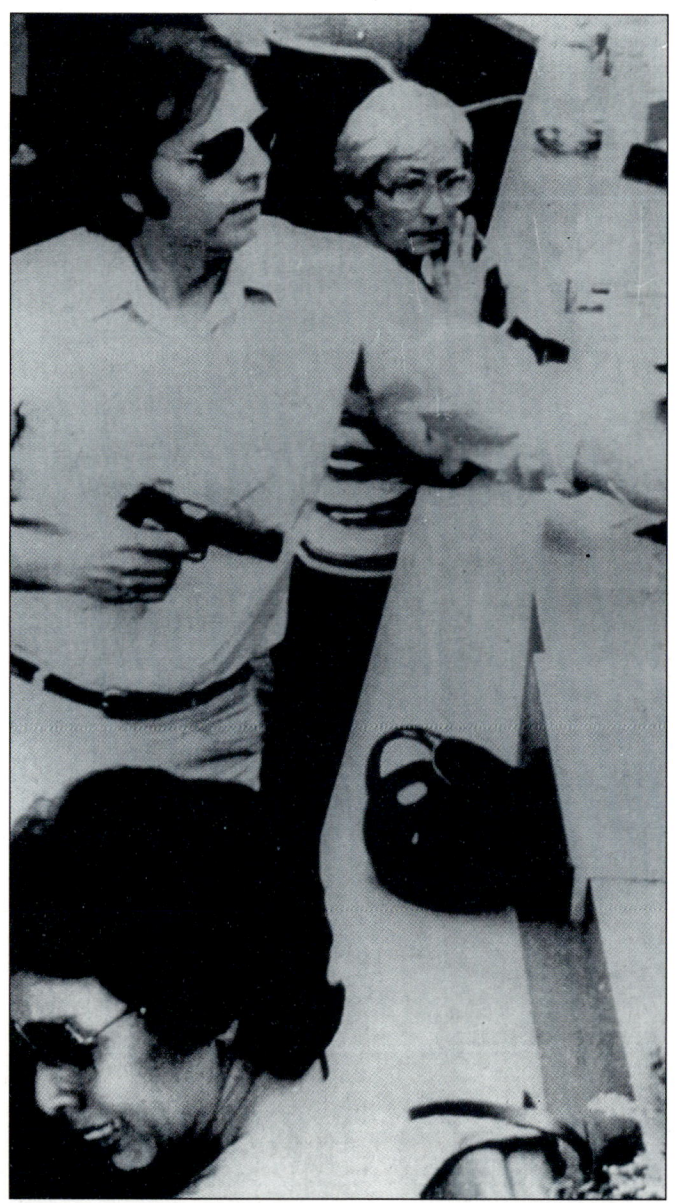

▼ In August 1981, this robbery in Indiana was photographed by the bank's security camera. Despite the picture, the robber was still unidentified a month later.

In the late 1930s, while Jacques Penry (1904–1987) was selecting the photographs for a book he had written called *Character from the Face*, he had the idea of compiling a photographic library of noses, eyes, chins, and so on. These could then be used as a resource to produce a photograph of a person. Known as Penry Facial Identification Technique (and later as Photo-FIT), Penry's system superseded the Identikit in 1971.

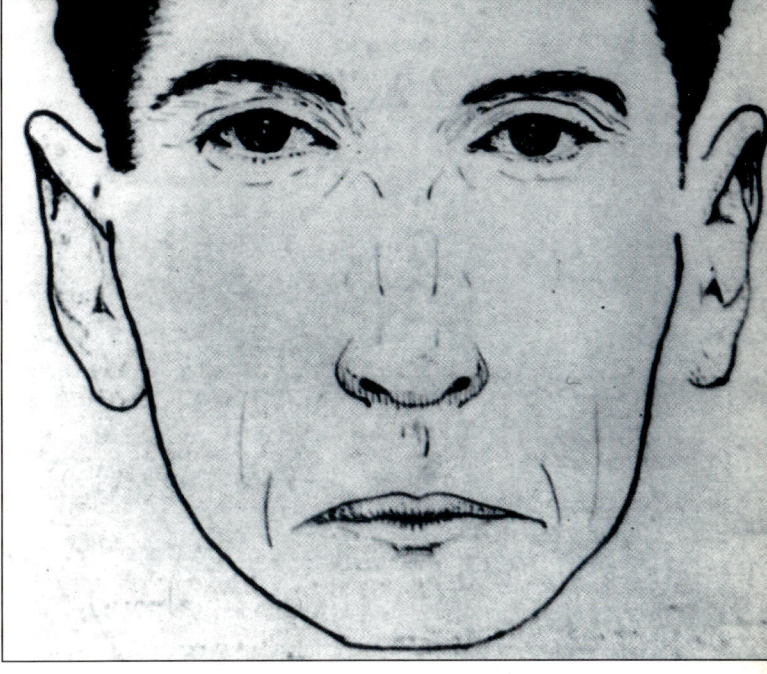

▲ Pictures of suspects, made up from descriptions provided by witnesses, are issued to newspapers by the police.

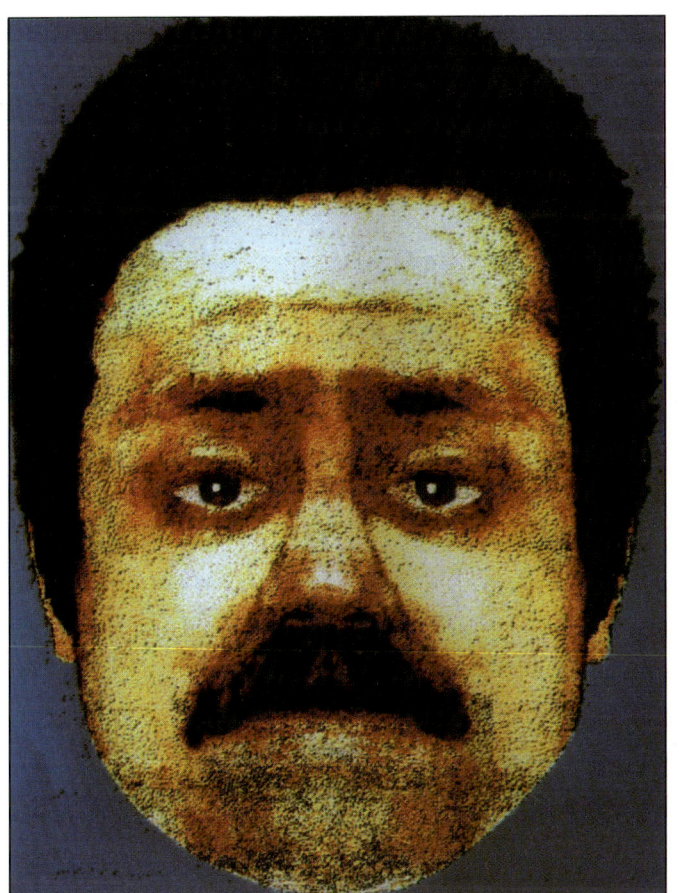

◄ An electronically generated picture of an unidentified man whose body was found on a railroad embankment near Leeds, England, in March 1995. Electronically generated images provide a more realistic picture, although there is still room for improvement in the technique.

During the 1980s and 1990s, Video Fit was developed. This is a procedure not unlike Photo-FIT, except the selection of facial characteristics is made into computer-generated images that can be subtly adjusted. Adjustments take into account minute observations and witness perceptions. Images are also produced with depth, color, and texture, thus adding to their realism. Similarly, the electronic enhancement of videotape taken by security cameras is becoming more commonplace, but it still needs refinement.

QUESTIONING

In the seventeenth century René Descartes (1596–1650), a French philosopher and physiologist, wrote the first scientific reports about automatic behavior in the human body, such as breathing, heartbeat, and so on. As part of his work, Descartes observed reflex actions. One typical reflex is blinking when a puff of air is directed into the eyes. In the eighteenth century Luigi Galvani (1737–1798), an Italian physiologist, showed that messages are carried from the brain to the muscles as electric currents running along the nerves. Although this current is weak, it is measurable. Galvani also noticed that when people are under stress, the electrical conductivity of the skin changes. This is known as galvanic skin response (GSR).

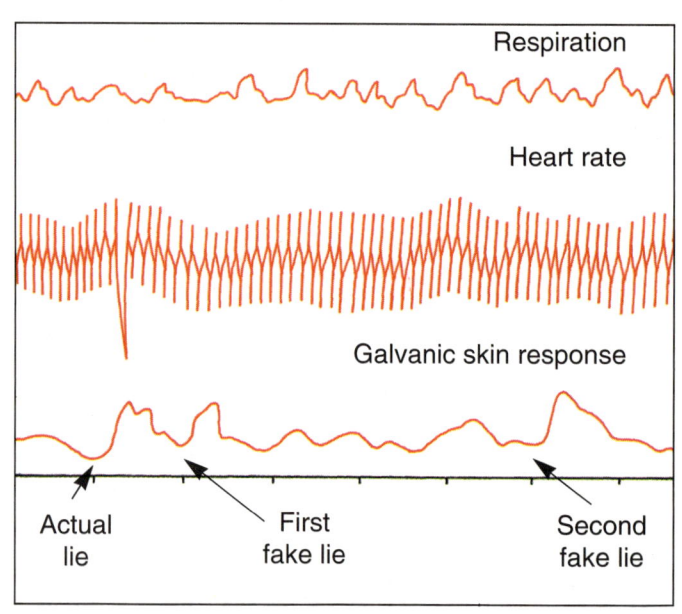

▲ A printout from a polygraph, or lie detector

▲ René Descartes was interested in many ideas besides the reflex actions of the human body.

These observations helped people understand the autonomic nervous system, which is a part of the larger central nervous system of human beings and other vertebrates. Some believe that changes in the autonomic nervous system occur when people tell lies. The polygraph is a device that measures changes that occur in GSR, heart rate, breathing patterns, and so on. The machine produces a record of these changes when the answer to a question is given.

Unfortunately, there are many, many ways of beating the machine, and many psychologists believe that this evidence is little better than guesswork. On the other hand, people who believe that the machine can detect lies and are frightened by it, do react when they tell lies. Some countries allow polygraph evidence to be given in court; many do not.

◀ Psychologists are trying to find reliable ways of helping people recall events. The techniques would be useful when investigating a crime to help witnesses remember things they have seen or heard.

Günter Köhenken in Germany and Ray Bull and Amina Memon in Great Britain were in 1995 conducting psychological research into ways in which witnesses may be helped to remember what they saw and heard at the scene of a crime.

In Florida and California, psychologists Ron Fisher and Ed Giesleman throughout the 1980s and 1990s have worked on a development called the cognitive interview. This is a series of techniques that people can use to remember events they think they have forgotten. For example, a witness says that at a bank robbery she or he heard one of the robbers say the name of an accomplice, but the person cannot remember that name. One technique is to ask the witness to run through the alphabet letter by letter. Sometimes this triggers the memory.

Smells are very strong cues to accessing memories, so another technique is to encourage the witnesses to think about any smells they might have sensed at the scene. People might also recall sounds, think about what the incident looked like from another position in the room, or try to remember things in reverse order. These and a number of other devices improve the accurate recall of incidents by as much as 40 percent or more.

CRIMINAL MINDS

Many years ago investigators realized that some criminals had systematic ways of committing their crimes. Edward Henry in Great Britain and Alphonse Bertillon in France encouraged their staff to keep records of criminal methods. To this day, most major police organizations around the world have a methods index in their criminal records office. This index helps identify criminals on the basis of their method of working.

Criminals who repeat similar types of offenses are called serial criminals. The most serious of these is the serial murderer. Today, police usually ask psychologists and psychiatrists to help them build a psychological sketch of the sort of person they are looking for. In the 1940s, during World War II (1939–1945), American psychiatrist William Langer produced a profile of the Nazi leader Adolf Hitler.

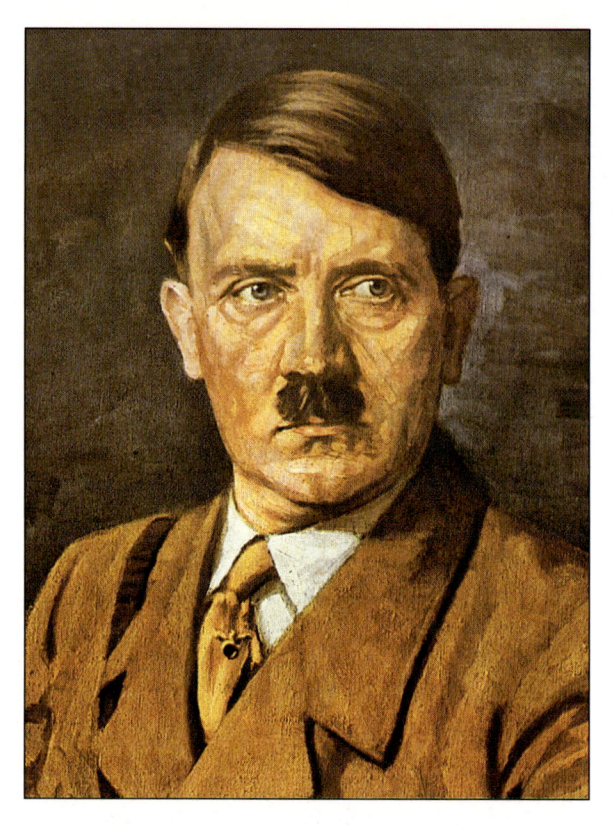

▲ During World War II, William Langer examined films, documents, and other records of Adolf Hitler. He discussed his subject with people who had met him. He was able to advise Allied commanders that Hitler was not only mentally unstable but also that he would probably kill himself if he lost the war. When Berlin was occupied, Hitler committed suicide. His badly burned body was identified through his dental records.

In 1957 James Brussell, another American psychiatrist, created a profile of a man known as the Mad Bomber, who for sixteen years had waged a terror campaign against the Consolidated Edison Company in New York City. Brussell's profile pinpointed the Mad Bomber as a single man between the ages of 40 and 50, unsociable but not antisocial, a skilled mechanic, and a high school graduate. When George Metsky was arrested, these and other suggestions in the profile were found to be true. Brussell also created a profile for the Boston Strangler—Albert de Salvo—who was arrested in 1964. Between 1962 and 1963, de Salvo had killed 11 women. Among other things found to be accurate in the profile, Brussell predicted that the offender would be around 30 years old and of Spanish or Italian descent.

Following the success of Brussell's work, the FBI Behavioral Science Unit was set up in the 1970s. Now known as the Violent Criminal Apprehension Program, it is made up of a group of FBI agents and behavioral scientists who have compiled a large computerized database of serial criminals and their crimes. This database is available to police forces throughout the world.

The approach to profiling that Brussell and many American profilers use involves matching the symptoms of a known psychological disorder to the crimes and then constructing the profile on the basis of what is known about people who suffer from such disorders.

◀ As well as providing the police with descriptions of serial killers, profiles are often employed when hostages are taken. Profiles are used to assess the behavior of the criminals and their hostages and to make predictions about the behavior of both if the police launch an attack.

Another method of profiling is the crime scene analysis approach. This is a variation of Locard's trace element approach to forensic science. David Canter (1944–) of Liverpool University, England, believes that everything that happens (or sometimes what does not happen) at the scene of a crime is significant in building a profile. Each tiny piece of evidence, both from the crime scene and from witnesses or victims, is of value and can be subjected to rigorous examination, often through computerized plotting techniques. Canter also believes that a serial criminal repeats strategies that have been successful and changes in predictable ways strategies that have not worked well.

GENETIC FINGERPRINTS

Gregor Johann Mendel (1822–1884), an Austrian monk, spent his life working in the monastery gardens growing peas. Mendel was interested in the ways in which one variety of pea plant, when fertilized by another, produced a new variety that had elements in common with each of the parent plants. This process is now called crossbreeding. In 1865 Mendel published a paper on his studies in crossbreeding dwarf and giant peas. In 1900 three botanists working separately rediscovered Mendel's laws, and in 1909 American zoologist Thomas Hunt Morgan (1866–1945) continued the work with fruit flies. In 1933 Morgan received a Nobel prize for establishing that heredity is passed on through the chromosomes. This is one of the basic principles of genetics.

▶ The basic genetic material found in cells is DNA. We now know that the DNA molecule has two strands wound around each other and is connected at regular intervals.

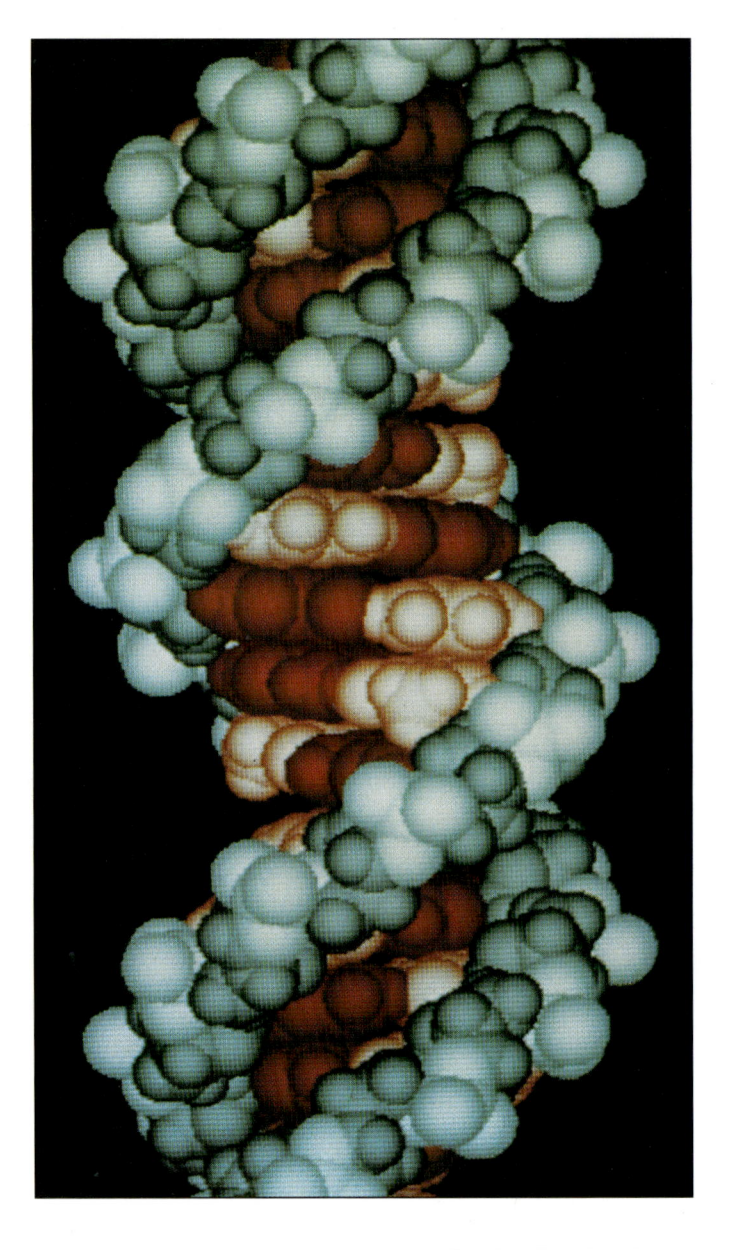

In 1962 James Watson (1928–), an American, and Francis Crick (1916–), an Englishman, shared a Nobel prize for their work at Cambridge University in discovering the structure of deoxyribonucleic acid, or DNA. DNA is contained within the billions of cells that make up the human body. It is a code that is unique to each of us and that also allows us to pass on some of our characteristics to our children.

The techniques of DNA profiling were developed in 1984 by Alec Jeffreys of the Lister Institute at Leicester University in Great Britain. Jeffreys discovered that DNA can be extracted from the blood and cut up using chemicals taken from certain types of bacteria, which are part of the body's natural defense system. If the DNA sample is placed in a special gel and an electric current is applied, the DNA fragments move through the gel. The presence and position of each fragment of the DNA sample on the gel make up the unique genetic fingerprint of its donor.

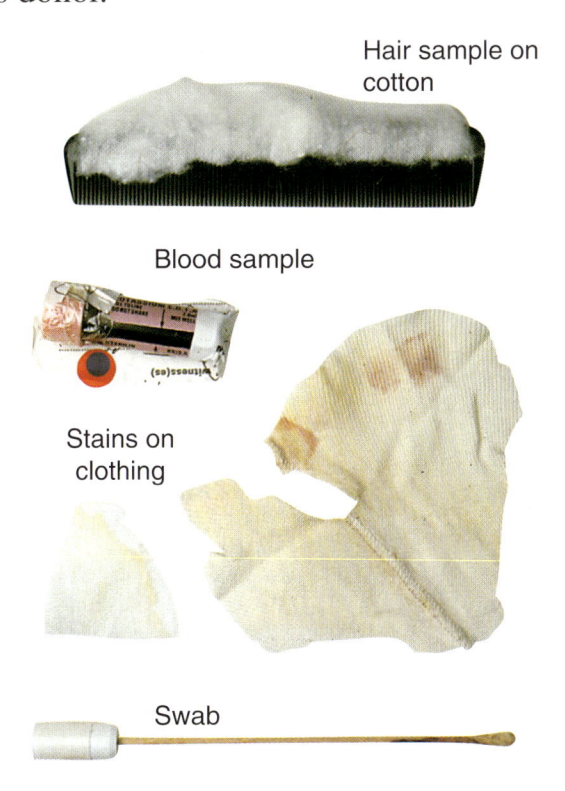

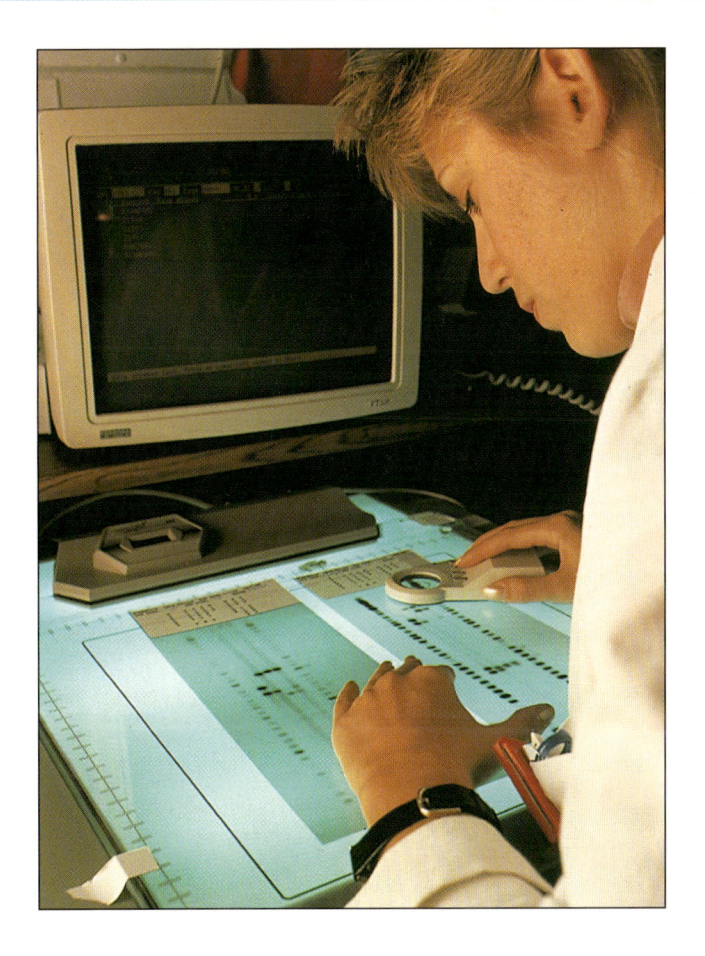

Hair sample on cotton

Blood sample

Stains on clothing

Swab

▲ At the forensic laboratory, details of genetic fingerprints are entered into a computer database. This aids identification and cross matching.

◀ At the crime scene, scientists collect evidence from which genetic fingerprints of the criminals can be produced, such as hair, dried blood, or sweat stains. A doctor may take swabs of bodily fluids from rape and assault victims.

Although some people may share one or two DNA similarities, it has been estimated that only two people in ten billion have identical complete DNA patterns (identical twins are excluded from this calculation as their DNA will be almost identical). Since calculations suggest that the population of the world is about five billion, it is assumed for most practical purposes that a person's genetic fingerprint is unique. Comparison of a DNA sample taken from the scene of a crime with that supplied by a suspect is considered valuable evidence of guilt or innocence. Jeffreys's first application of the technique in 1983 showed that a man suspected of two murders, one of which he had confessed to, was innocent of both.

DATABASES

In 1833 Charles Babbage (1792–1871), who had been Professor of Mathematics at Cambridge University, made what is usually thought of as the world's first computer. The machine, called the difference engine, was made from precisely machined brass parts. There was no understanding of electronics at that time, and it was not until 1941 that Konrad Zuse, a German, produced a device that worked on the basis of a program that was stored within the machine.

▲ The Macintosh Performa 630CD computer (with a 500 MB internal hard disk and up to 52 MB of random access memory) is far more powerful than the first vacuum tube computers and occupies a fraction of the space.

▲ This false-color picture, taken by an electron microscope, shows part of the integrated circuit on a silicon chip. The colors relate to different electronic pathways on the surface of the chip. Each indentation on a blue pathway is a single transistor memory cell. The magnification shown here is about 3,000 times the original.

Early electronic computers were huge, sometimes filling a series of rooms. In 1946 a team of electronics experts at the University of Pennsylvania completed a machine called ENIAC. It contained 18,000 vacuum tubes and filled a large room. In 1948, three American scientists, William Shockley (1910–1989), John Bardeen (1908–1991), and Walter Brattain (1902–1987) designed the first transistor (a kind of miniature vacuum tube). Later, in 1959, integrated circuits on silicon chips were developed by a team of American scientists. These contain many transistors on small wafers of silicon. Even the simpler modern computers, based on silicon chip technology, are more powerful than the vacuum tube-based machines.

▶ More than three hundred people were killed on December 22, 1988 when a bomb exploded on Pan Am flight 103 over Lockerbie, Scotland. The British police collected, numbered, listed, and bagged all the pieces of wreckage. This was the beginning of a major international investigation to identify and bring to justice those responsible. Airline security procedures throughout the world were tightened after investigators discovered how the bomb was hidden on the plane.

◀ On November 14, 1991, Abdel Basset Ali al-Megrahi, seen here entering the Supreme Court in Tripoli, Libya, was one of two Libyans charged with the bombing of Pan Am flight 103.

One major feature of modern law enforcement and crime investigation is computerized data, and there is a growing need for it to be available to police officers and their support staff, both on a local and on a worldwide basis. Local in-force computer systems are common and information about crime and criminals can be passed rapidly from place to place. There is a growing number of international agreements that are not restricted by national borders. In Europe, for example, the Schengen Information System (named after the small city in which the agreement was signed) currently involves only a handful of countries, but it is providing the basis for a fully integrated European information system on crime. Most countries in the world have similar systems.

There is, however, nothing new about the sharing of crime and investigation information among nations. For more than 50 years the Interpol (International Police) organization, which has its headquarters in Paris, France, has acted as a coordinating body for international crime investigations. Contrary to popular belief, Interpol does not investigate crime; it merely acts as the channel through which information is passed. It seems highly likely, however, that an international investigative body will gradually develop to counteract worldwide crime.

CHRONOLOGY OF ADVANCE

Here are some of the people, discoveries, inventions, and improvements that have helped shape methods of criminal investigation used today.

Ancient Babylon The code of Hammurabi was an important law in ancient Babylon (eighteenth century B.C.). It was very harsh. If, for example, one man accused another of murder but could not prove it, the accuser was executed.

Roman law Roman law (753 B.C.–A.D. 235) was very precise and often written down. The first law book was published about 200 B.C.

Mosaic law This was law based on religious doctrine, including the Ten Commandments (about 1100 B.C.–A.D. 300). It later developed into the Torah, the Mishnah, and the Gemara. Much of the law was administered by rabbis.

Middle Ages In the period A.D. 500–1500, legal systems were largely destroyed. Punishments and trials were harsh and unreasonable.

Marcello Malpighi An Italian physiologist (1628–1694) who noticed the patterns on the tips of human fingers.

Antoni van Leeuwenhoek A Dutch scientist (1632–1723) who in 1670 built the first effective microscope.

Luigi Galvani An Italian physiologist (1737–1798) who established that information is transmitted electrically through the nervous system. This observation is the basis for lie-detection equipment.

Matthieu Orfila A Spanish chemist (1787–1853) who published a system for classifying poisons in 1814. It is still the basis of forensic toxicology.

Jan Evangelista Purkinje A Czechoslovakian physiologist (1787–1869) who described the ridges and grooves on the skin of the fingers.

Robert Peel A British politician (1788–1850) who on September 29, 1829, was responsible for the first fully functional civilian police: the London Metropolitan Police.

▲ Luigi Galvani

▲ Antoni van Leeuwenhoek

Henry Faulds A Scottish physiologist (1843–1930) who in the 1870s published a paper describing dactylography, an early form of fingerprinting.

Francis Galton An English scientist (1822–1911) who in 1892 described the four basic delta patterns of fingerprints.

Cesare Lombroso An Italian criminologist (1836–1909) who in 1876 proposed that the physical features of people indicated particular types of criminal activity. He also suggested that most criminals, because their physical appearance determined their behavior, were incapable of avoiding a life of crime. This idea has since been discredited.

William Herschel An English civil servant (1833–1917) who developed a fingerprinting system to prevent fraud by retired soldiers in India.

Thomas Hunt Morgan An American physiologist (1866–1945) who in 1909 established that heredity is passed on through the chromosomes, confirming one of the basic principles of genetics.

Alexandre Lacassagne A French criminologist (1844–1921) who was the father of forensic science. Among his numerous discoveries he pointed out that rifling inside a gun's barrel leaves unique marks on the bullets fired from the gun. He also suggested that bloodstains and blood marks at the scene of a crime leave evidence of what happened during the crime.

Wilhelm Conrad Röntgen A German physicist (1845-1923) who discovered X rays. X rays are now used in forensic dentistry, in fingerprint examination, and in the examination of documents.

Alphonse Bertillon A French criminologist (1853–1914) who developed a system to identify criminals from their body measurements. This became known as the Bertillon system.

Edward Henry An English criminologist (1859–1931) who finalized the classification of fingerprints. In 1901 he became director of the fingerprint branch at Scotland Yard in London.

Karl Landsteiner An Austrian biologist (1868–1943) who in 1901 identified blood antigens (A and B), enabling blood to be classified.

▲ Alexandre Lacassagne

Edmond Locard A French doctor and lawyer (1877–1966) who had been a student of Alexandre Lacassagne at the University of Lyons. In 1910 he published his ideas about the exchange principle.

Vladimir Zworykin A Russian physicist (1889-1982) who designed and developed the scanning electron microscope, which enabled images to be magnified up to 150,000 times.

Jacques Penry A photographer (1904–1987) who developed a method that allowed witnesses to put together photographs of facial features to create the full face. Now called Photo-FIT, it replaced the line drawings used by Identikit.

Keith Simpson A British forensic pathologist (1907–1988) who was responsible for many developments of forensic science, including those of forensic odontology (dentistry) and pathology. He was involved in many famous British criminal cases.

William Shockley An American physicist (1910–1989) who, with **John Bardeen** and **Walter Brattain**, developed the first transistor in 1948. This small device replaced bulky electronic vacuum tubes, allowing rapid developments in electronic engineering and computer technology.

Theodore Maiman An American physicist (1927–) who designed the first laser. Laser light, which is concentrated pure light, can be used to reveal fingerprints. It has many other commercial and medical applications.

James Watson An American scientist (1928–) who, with his English colleague **Francis Crick** (1916–), was responsible for the identification and description of the structure of DNA. This work underpinned the development of genetic fingerprinting in 1984.

Robert Freeman A British engineer (1946–) who, with **Douglas Foster** (1946–), designed the the Electro-Static Document Apparatus (ESDA). ESDA allows impressions left on paper to be enhanced and examined.

David Canter A British scientist (1944–) who is the principal researcher into the "crime scene analysis" approach to offender profiling. Canter believes that everything that happens at the scene of a crime can scientifically assist in building a psychological profile of the suspect.

GLOSSARY

Antibody A molecule produced by the body to fight infection and other invading substances.

Antigen A substance (usually a protein) that is recognized by and attacked by antibodies.

Anthropology The study of human beings, their structure, evolution, and their culture and organization.

Ballistics The science of projectiles of firearms. This is not the same as firearms identification, which matches bullets with the guns that have fired them.

Bertillon system An identification system devised by Alphonse Bertillon, which is based on the idea that each individual's body measurements are different. Investigators could compare details of a suspect with those held on file.

Blood types Medical researchers developed a way to classify blood into types. The classification allows forensic scientists to say (within varying degrees of certainty) whether or not blood comes from a particular person. The main types are A, B, AB, and O. These may be rhesus (Rh) positive or negative.

Chromatography A technique used to separate a substance into its components. Components move through an apparatus at different speeds. As each one passes a sensor it produces an electrical charge that can be recorded.

Chromosome A threadlike structure found in the nucleus of a cell. It is made up of DNA and protein arranged in the genes. Genes are the units of inheritance. Each species has characteristic genes and chromosomes.

Cognitive interview A series of memory-enhancing techniques. It is increasingly used by police officers to improve the quality and quantity of information obtained by witnesses to crimes.

Comparison microscope Two microscopes connected by an arrangement of mirrors, allowing two objects to be compared in a single eyepiece. Although developed to help compare bullets, it has a wide range of applications in forensic science.

Criminal type The classification by Cesare Lombroso of physical characteristics that dictate criminal behavior. The notion has no scientific foundation.

Dactylography An early name for the study of fingerprints.

▼ **Amina Memon, one of the researchers who in 1995 was working on cognitive interview techniques**

Daguerreotype A forerunner of the modern photograph. It was necessary for the subjects to stand motionless, often for some minutes. The slightest movement produced a blurred picture. For some portrait photographs, people had their heads clamped with semicircles of metal behind their necks.

DNA Deoxyribonucleic acid (DNA), the substance found in the nucleus of cells. DNA is the genetic code that makes all living things, including human beings, different from one another.

Electron microscope The scanning electron microscope uses a beam of electrons to provide images up to 150,000 times larger than their true size. Images can be viewed on a computer screen or produced as photographs. The procedure is very useful in forensic examination because it does not damage the sample and other tests can follow without fear of contamination (*see* **Exchange principle**).

Emission spectroscopy When a substance burns, it emits light that is typical of the components of the substance. Passing this light through a prism produces a spectrum by which the components can be analyzed. By comparing the spectrum from an unknown substance with data obtained from control samples, the substance can be accurately identified. This technique is called emission spectroscopy.

Exchange principle "Every contact leaves a trace" is the key feature of almost all forensic science. People leave traces of themselves at crime scenes, and these traces attach themselves to clothing, shoes, hands, and so on. This applies to criminals and investigators alike. Investigators must take special precautions to ensure they do not contaminate evidence.

Fingerprint classification Most scientific techniques rely on classifying, retrieving, and identifying data. Fingerprint classification depends upon standard and identifiable patterns, which occur in one way or another in all fingerprints. The standard patterns are arches, loops, whorls, and deltas (or triangles).

Fingerprints Fingerprint experts use the term *ink fingerprints* for the print records made following an arrest. This is to distinguish them from the prints found at a crime scene, which are called *evidence fingerprints*.

▲ The FBI serology laboratory in Washington, D.C., is typical of many forensic laboratories. Samples of bodily fluids taken from suspects or crime scenes are sent here for analysis.

Forensic scientists Investigators who use scientific methods to provide evidence of the guilt or innocence of a person charged with a crime. Forensic laboratories are usually used only for forensic investigation.

Galvanic skin response The measurable change in the electrical conductance of the skin. It forms part of the measurements taken by the polygraph, or lie detector.

Identikit A series of line drawings of facial features, which in combination produce a likeness of a person described by a witness. Now superseded by Photo-FIT and Video Fit.

Laser A device that sends out a very intense, narrow beam of light of pure color. The light beam is extremely powerful and can be focused very accurately.

45

Mass spectrometry An analysis technique that measures the mass of each component in a compound or mixture. The sample is bombarded with electrons to charge particles that can then be separated by electric and magnetic fields. A trace is recorded on paper and displayed on a computer screen with peaks for each of the components present. The trace is called a mass spectrum.

Offender profiling An assessment made by a psychologist or psychiatrist of an unidentified person who commits a series of similar crimes. The assessment considers the person's character and possible background and aims to predict future criminal behavior.

Paleontology The study of life in past geological periods.

Pathology The science of diseases that affect the human body.

Photo-FIT A series of photographs of facial features that can be combined to produce a likeness of a person described by a witness.

Physiology The science of the functions and phenomena of living organisms.

Police The body of people employed to ensure that the citizens keep the peace and obey the law. In many countries there is a tradition of civilian policing, but in some countries the police are part of the army and are government-controlled. In a few countries, both forms exist.

▶ British police supported by other emergency services begin the investigation after a terrorist bomb exploded in the financial district of London in April 1992.

▶ Tokyo police help a young boy find his way through the city streets.

Polygraph A lie detector that takes measurements of bodily changes such as galvanic skin response (GSR), heart rate, and respiration rate. The person analyzing the resulting trace makes judgments about whether or not responses to questions are lies or truths.

Psychiatry The study and treatment of mental disease.

Psychology The science of the human mind.

Rifling Grooves on the inside of a gun barrel that produce greater accuracy because they cut into the soft metal of the bullet and make it spin. Rifling marks on bullets are unique to the weapon from which the bullets were fired.

Serial crime Repeated criminal activity by the same person.

Trajectory The path made by a bullet after it has been fired from a gun. The study of ballistics is the examination of the possible trajectories of bullets. The path depends upon a number of factors that include the type of weapon used, the nature of the ammunition, the distance of the shooter from the target, the weather (for example, wind speed), and the nature of the material through which the bullet passes.

Trial by ordeal A system used in Europe in the Middle Ages to decide whether a person was guilty or innocent of a crime. People often died in the course of the ordeal.

Ultraviolet light Lightlike radiation that is invisible to the human eye. Certain substances shine brightly when bathed in ultraviolet light. Forensic scientists use these substances to reveal marks that would otherwise go undetected.

X rays Radiationlike light with a wavelength that is even shorter than ultraviolet light. X rays pass through some materials (for example, human flesh) but are reflected or absorbed by others (for example, bone and lead). Photographic images can be produced of the materials through which the X rays do not pass.

FURTHER READING

Nonfiction

Gardner, Robert. *Crime Lab 101: Experimenting with Crime Detection*. New York: Walker & Co., 1992.

Graham, Ian. *Crime-Fighting*. Science Spotlight. Milwaukee: Raintree Steck-Vaughn, 1995.

Israel, Fred L. *The Federal Bureau of Investigation*. Know Your Government. New York: Chelsea House, 1986.

Lampton, Christopher. *DNA Fingerprinting*. Impact Books. New York: Franklin Watts, 1991.

Place, Robin. *Bodies from the Past*. Digging up the Past. New York: Thomson Learning, 1995.

Tesar, Jenny. *Scientific Crime Investigation*. Venture Books. New York: Franklin Watts, 1991.

Winters, Paul A., ed. *Crime and Criminals: Opposing Viewpoints*. San Diego: Greenhaven Press, 1995.

Fiction for older readers

Patricia D. Cornwell, who worked in a Medical Examiner's office, is the author of a number of murder mysteries that deal with the work of a Forensic Medical Examiner in Richmond, Virginia. Through the character of Dr. Kay Scarpetta, Chief Medical Examiner, the author relays a wealth of information about the techniques of forensic science. The books so far are: *Postmortem, Body of Evidence, Cruel and Unusual, All that Remains, The Body Farm,* and *From Potter's Field*. Some scenes in the books are very graphic. They are not recommended for readers who are squeamish. The books are available in paperback from Avon Books.

INDEX

Numbers in **bold** refer to pictures or drawings as well as text.

Aston, Francis 26

Babbage, Charles 40
ballistics 20, 21, 44
Bertillon, Alphonse **11**, 15, 36, 43
Bertillon system **11**, 44
blood **21**, **22**, **23**, **26**, 27, **39**, 44
bombs 36, **41**, **46–47**
Boston Strangler 36
Bragg
　William Henry 17
　William Lawrence 17
Brussell, James 36, 37
Bull, Ray 35
Bunsen, Robert 23
Burrard, Gerald 21

Canter, David 37, 43
chromatography **22–23**, 44
cognitive interviews **35**, 44
Colt, Samuel **19**
computers **16**, **17**, 20, **22–23**, **26–27**, 31, 33, 37, **39**, **40**, 41
Connally, John 21
corpses 12, **28**, **29**, 30
Crick, Francis 38, 43
criminals 9, 10, **11**, 16, **32**, 36, **37**, **39**
criminal types **10**

dactylography 11, 44
Daguerre, Louis **7**, 45
daguerreotype 7, 45
de Salvo, Albert 36
death sentence 16
Descartes, René **34**
DNA 38, 39, 45
dogs **7**
ducking stool **6**

Egyptian mummy 26

ENIAC 40
ESDA 25
evidence 4, **5**, **9**, 13, 16, 34, 37, **39**
exchange principle 4, 9, 19, 23
executions 6, 10, 26

Faulds, Henry 15, 43
FBI **21**, 37, **45**
fingerprints 11, **14**, **15**, **16**, **17**, 24, 45
Fischer, John 20
Fisher, Ron 35
forensic 5
　anthropologists 28
　dentistry 12–13
　investigation 4
　laboratories **5**, **20**, **21**, **39**, **45**
　science 7, 9, 31, 37, 44
　scientists 4, 5, 7, 9, **20**, **21**, 23, 24, **25**, 26, 45
Foster, Douglas 25
Freeman, Robert 25, 43

Galton, Francis 15, 42
Galvani, Luigi 34, **42**
genetic fingerprinting **5**, 38, **39**
Gerasimov, Mikhail 30, 31
Giesleman, Ed 35
Glaister, John 23
Goddard, Calvin 20
Gorringe, George 13
Graham, Daniel 17, 24
Gravelle, Philip 20
Gray, Hugh 17, 24
guns 9, **18**, **19**, **20**, **21**

Haigh, John George 13
handwriting **24**, **25**
Harvey, William 22
Henry, Edward 15, 16, 17, 36, 43
Herschel, William 14, 15, 42

Hitler, Adolf 36
hostages 37
Huygens, Christiaan 24

Iceman **29**, **30–31**
Identikit 32, **33**, 45

Jackson, Harry 16
Jeffreys, Alec 39
Jennings, Thomas 16

Kennedy, John F. 13, 21
Kirchhoff, Gustav 23
Knoll, Max 12
Köhenken, Günter 35

Lacassagne, Alexandre 19, 23, **43**
Landsteiner, Karl 22, 43
Langer, William 36
laser 17, 31, 45
Leeuwenhoek, Antoni van 7, **42**
Locard, Edmond 9, 19, 23, 24, 37, 43
Lombroso, Cesare 10, 42

Maiman, Theodore 17, 43
Malpighi, Marcello 14, 42
Marsh, James 26
mass spectrometer **26–27**, 46
McDonald, Hugh 32
McKern, Thomas 28
mechanical fit 7
Memon, Amina 35, **44**
Mendel, Gregor Johann 38
Messiter, Vivian 25
Metsky, George 36
microscopes 7
　comparison **20**, 24
　electron **cover**, **12–13**, **40**, 45
Morgan, Thomas Hunt 12, 38, 42
murders **12**, 13, 16, 18, 19, 30, 36, 39

Neave, Richard 30
Newton, Isaac 23
Nobel, Alfred 19
Nobel prizes 17, 19, 26, 38

Orfila, Matthieu 26, 42

Peel, Robert **8**, 42
Penry, Jacques 33, 43
Photo–FIT 33, 45, 46
Podmore, William 25
police **4–5**, 6, **8–9**, 15, 36, 37, 41, **46**
polygraphs **34**, 46
profiles 36, 37, 46
　DNA **39**
Purkinje, Jan Evangelista 14, 42

Richards, Robin 31
Ritter, Johann 24
robberies **32**, 35
Röntgen, Wilhelm Conrad 17, 43
Ruska, Ernst 12

Schultz, Johann 7
security cameras **32**, 33
Shockley, William 40, 43
silicon chip **40**
Simpson, Keith **12**, 13, 43
skulls **30–31**
Stewart, Thomas 28

Taylor, Alfred 26
teeth **12–13**, 29, **36**

Video Fit 33, 45

Waite, Charles 20
Watson, James 38, 43

X rays 17, 24, 47

Zuse, Konrad 40
Zworykin, Vladimir 12, 43

DISCARDED
Goshen Public Library

J
363.25
MACK

McKenzie, Ian K.
The history of criminal investigation